<u>Marlborough's Self-Taught Series</u>

ARABIC SELF-TAUGHT

(Syrian)

MARLBOROUGH'S SELF-TAUGHT SERIES

ARABIC SELF-TAUGHT

(Syrian)

WITH

English Phonetic Pronunciation

By

A. Hassam

ENLARGED AND REVISED BY

The Rev. N. Odeh,

Late Chaplain to the Rt. Rev. G.F.P. Blyth. D.D. Bishop in Jerusalem

GYAN

Published by

GYAN

Gyan Publishing House
5, Ansari Road
Darayaganj, New Delhi-110002
Phone: 011-47034999, 9811692060
E-mail: books@gyanbooks.com

Distribution Network
gyanbooks.com
India, USA, Canada, UK, Australia, France

ISBN : 978-81-212-4245-5 (PB)
First Published, 1915

2nd Impression 2020

Printed at: Gyan Press, Delhi.

The book at your disposal is the edition of an old book originally published long back. The Text quality of this book may not be at par as compared to our other books but many readers approached us to reprint this important book so that it could satiate their hunger. We request all the readers of this book to help us to improve its quality by providing the necessary text of those pages which are not properly visible. Your valuable support in this case will be highly appreciated and acknowledged and our future readers will be benefitted immensely.

Marlborough's Self-Taught Series.

Arabic Self-Taught.

(Syrian.)

With

English Phonetic Pronunciation.

By

A. Hassam.

Enlarged and revised by

The Rev. N. Odeh,

Late Chaplain to the Rt. Rev. G. F. P. Blyth, D.D., Bishop in Jerusalem.

Fifth Edition.

E. MARLBOROUGH & CO., 51 OLD BAILEY, LONDON, E.C.

1915.

PREFACE.

THE present enlarged edition of *Arabic Self-Taught* is to all intents and purposes a new work. It has practically been re-written throughout and much entirely new matter has been added, whilst those portions of the original English text that have been retained have undergone thorough revision with a view to adapting them to modern requirements.

The Vocabularies and Conversations have been carefully selected for practical use in the daily life of tourists, travellers, missionaries, business men, and all who come into contact with the natives of Syria. The work forms an easy guide to spoken (colloquial) Arabic, and gives the student a practical and valuable introduction to the thorough study of the language.

The system of transliteration here employed, carefully devised to give the phonetic pronunciation of Arabic in accordance with the scheme adopted by the Congress of Orientalists, has been simplified to the last degree, and the key to the vowel sounds, diphthongs, and hard consonants, given at the foot of the pages throughout the Vocabularies and Conversations, will greatly facilitate the intelligible pronunciation of the Arabic words at sight.

The new outline of grammar throws much useful light upon the construction of Arabic, and the exercises which follow contain abundant conversational matter illustrative of the grammatical rules. The student can thus obtain an intelligent grasp of the words and sentences he learns by heart, and make them his own.

In carrying out the work of revision the Publishers have had the assistance of the Rev. N. Odeh, who spent many years in Palestine and Egypt as a missionary and Head Master of St. Mary's School, Cairo, and has since been engaged in teaching Arabic at Oxford.

At first sight Arabic letters appear very difficult to learn, and this is partly the reason why students and travellers fight shy of the language; but Eastern tongues are not difficult to acquire by the 'SELF-TAUGHT' method, and any ordinary capacity can master them in a short time. The student or traveller, thus becoming his own *Dragoman*, will more thoroughly enjoy a sojourn in the East.

The best plan for a beginner to adopt is to copy each letter carefully and repeatedly, until he has fixed it in his mind; for this purpose only two or three letters should be dealt with at a time, and not the whole alphabet. He will be surprised to find how soon he begins to understand the characters in their various positions.

Having mastered the alphabet, he may proceed to commit to memory the words given in the vocabularies, pronouncing the phonetic aloud, and then writing the words from memory in the Arabic letters, which can be corrected afterwards by reference to the book. In this way he will begin to acquire the language as easily as a child learns to speak and write its native tongue.

At the same time it may be borne in mind that, if this manual is merely required as a phrase-book, the labour of learning the Arabic characters is really unnecessary, as most Arabs with whom one comes in contact are quite unable to read the language.

When travelling it is well to note the sound of the words uttered by the natives, as this helps one to attach the true value to the phonetics used, and accustoms the ear to the gutturals and soft aspirants of the Eastern tongue.

The written or classic Arabic is beautifully constructed. It belongs to the Semitic languages, which include, amongst others, Hebrew, Chaldee, and Syriac. It has indeed survived all the other Semitic languages, and is the most exact in its use of the original root. Many common household words of modern Arabs are not merely similar to, but identical with, those of the ancient Hebrews, and it is not too much to say that an Israelite of old and an Arab Sheikh of the present day would be mutually intelligible in the expression of their simple wants.

London, 1911.

CONTENTS.

ARABIC SELF-TAUGHT.

The Alphabet and Pronunciation.

The following scheme of pronunciation is the key to the correct reading of the Arabic words throughout the work, and the student will do well, therefore, to give careful attention to it at the outset, repeatedly copying each character *together with its phonetic transcription*, until the eye and the mind become so familiar with them that the character immediately suggests the sound.

The method of distinguishing the hard consonants, *ḥ*, *ḍ*, *ṣ*, *ṭ*, and *ẓ*, is so simple that these letters will present no difficulty to the student, and the vowel sounds and diphthongs are equally easy to master. The key to all these sounds, given in the footlines on each page of the Vocabularies and Conversational Sentences, will enable any English-speaking person to pronounce the words correctly at sight.

The Arabic alphabet is composed of twenty-eight consonants, all of which are written, as in most Eastern languages, from the right hand to the left. Each consonant assumes a different form according to its position at the beginning, middle, or end of the word. On the next two pages the various forms are placed in separate columns and show how each character is written respectively—

When totally unconnected with any other letter;

When at the end of a word, or joined only to the letter preceding;

When connected with the preceding and following letters;

When at the beginning of a word, or joined only to the letter following.

The Forms of the Letters.

Name.	Unconnected Characters.	Connected with preceding letter only.	Connected on both sides.	Connected with following letter only.	Transcription.
Alif . .	ا	ـا	—	—	a, i, u
Bā . .	ب	ـب	ـبـ	بـ	b
Tā . .	ت	ـت	ـتـ	تـ	t
Thā . .	ث	ـث	ـثـ	ثـ	th
Jeem . .	ج	ـج	ـجـ	جـ	j
Ḥā . .	ح	ـح	ـحـ	حـ	ḥ
Khā . .	خ	ـخ	ـخـ	خـ	kh
Dāl . .	د	ـد	—	—	d
Dhāl . .	ذ	ـذ	—	—	dh
Rā . .	ر	ـر	—	—	r
Zā, zai, *or* zain	ز	ـز	—	—	z
Seen . .	س	ـس	ـسـ	سـ	s
Sheen . .	ش	ـش	ـشـ	شـ	sh
Ṣād . .	ص	ـص	ـصـ	صـ	ṣ
Ḍād . .	ض	ـض	ـضـ	ضـ	ḍ

Name.	Unconnected Characters.	Connected with preceding letter only.	Connected on both sides.	Connected with following letter only.	Transcription.
Ṭā . .	ط	ـط	ـطـ	طـ	ṭ
Ẓā . .	ظ	ـظ	ـظـ	ظـ	ẓ
Ain . .	ع	ـع	ـعـ	عـ	'
Ghain . .	غ	ـغ	ـغـ	غـ	gh
Fā . .	ف	ـف	ـفـ	فـ	f
Qāf . .	ق	ـق	ـقـ	قـ	q
Kāf . .	ك ک	ـک	ـکـ ـگـ	کـ گـ	k
Lām . .	ل	ـل	ـلـ	لـ	l
Meem . .	م	ـم	ـمـ	مـ	m
Noon . .	ن	ـن	ـنـ	نـ	n
Hā . .	ه	ـه	ـهـ	هـ	h
Waw . .	و	ـو	—	—	w, ū
Yā . .	ی	ـی	ـیـ	یـ	y, ī

The letters ا د ذ ر ز and و can only be joined to those letters which precede.

From ل and ا *lām-alif* are formed لا or لا, in connexion ـلا.

From ن (*n*) and خ (*kh*) is formed the ligature نخ.

From ا (*a*) and ک (*k*) is formed the ligature کا.

Other ligatures are عج جح etc., etc.

Pronunciation of the Arabic Letters.

ا *Alif* has no sound of its own, but is pronounced as *a*, *i*, o *u*, according to the vowel above or below it. Whe not vowelled it is only a sign lengthening the pre ceding vowel.

ب *Bā* like the English *b*.

ت *Tā* like the English *t*.

ث *Thā* like the English *th* in 'thought'; it is often pro nounced like *t*.

ج *Jeem* like *j* in 'jam'; in Egypt hard like *g* in 'garden

ح *Ḥā* is always a strong aspirate with friction.

خ *Khā* is a guttural aspirate like *ch* in the German *ich* or th Scotch word 'loch'; *kh* always represents one sounc

د *Dāl* like the English *d*.

ذ *Dhāl* like *th* in 'that'; *dh* is always one sound.

ر *Rā* like *r* in 'rural', always sounded.

ز *Zā*, *zai*, or *zain* like the English *z*.

س *Seen* like *s* in 'some'.

ش *Sheen* like *sh* in 'sheep'.

ص *Ṣād* like a hard hissing *s* as in 'hiss'.

ض *Ḍāḍ* like a hard *d*, as in 'rod'.

ط *Ṭā* like a hard *t*, as in 'toss'.

ظ *Ẓā* like a dental *z*.

ع *Ain* is a guttural, peculiar to the Semitic languages, whic can only be learned by ear; it sounds like the bleatin of a goat (*māā*). When it begins a syllable we sha denote it by a *spiritus asper* (ʿ) before a vowel, ʿ when silent after a vowel.

غ *Ghain* a hard guttural produced as in the effort of garglin and sounds similar to *ghr*.

ف *Fā* like the English *f*.

ق *Qāf* like a broad *k*, produced as in imitating the cawing of a crow.

ك ك *Kāf* like the English *k*.

ل *Lām* like the English *l*.

م *Meem* like the English *m*.

ن *Noon* like the English *n*.

ه *Hā* like *h* in 'house'; if used as a grammatical termination it has two dots over it (ة), and has the sound of *t* when followed by a word beginning with vowel sound.

و *Waw* has the sound of the *w* in 'water', or of *u* in 'put'.

ي *Yā* sounds like *y* in 'yard'.

When و and ي are not vowelled, they are then only signs of lengthening the preceding vowel, *u* or *i*, or of making the diphthongs *au* and *ai* respectively.

Vowels and Orthographic Signs.

The Arabs use three signs to express short vowels, which are placed either above or below the consonants, namely—

(ـَ) *Fatha*, an oblique line over the consonant, represents *a* in 'hat'.

(ـِ) *Kasra*, an oblique line under the consonant, represents *i* in 'hit'.

(ـُ) *Damma*, represents *u* in 'put'.

Silent ا after ـَ makes the long vowel *ā* (as *a* in 'father'), e.g. مَا *mā* (water).

Silent ي after ـِ makes the long vowel *ī* (as *i* in 'machine'), e.g. فِي *fī* (in).

Silent و after ـُ makes the long vowel *ū* (as *u* in 'rule'), e.g. ذُو *dhū* (possessor).

Silent و after ـَ makes the diphthong *ou* (as *ow* in 'cow'), e.g. لَو *lau* (if).

Silent ي after ـَ makes the diphthong *ai* (as *ai* in 'aisle'), e.g. شَي *shai* (thing).

The vowel is always sounded after, never before the consonant with which it is written.

The other reading signs used in Arabic are—

ـْ *Jazmah*, placed over a letter that has no vowel.

ـٓ *Maddah*, a sign of prolongation over the ا.

ـٱ *Waslah*, placed over ا to denote that it forms one syllable with the preceding consonant.

ـّ *Shaddah*, signifies doubling a letter.

ـٔ *Hamzah*, placed over the ا where it is a sounded guttural consonant—transcribed '.

[N.B. It is not usual to mark all the vowels or signs in writing Arabic; in a newspaper or book very few, if any, are marked.]

Rules for the Pronunciation of the Vowels.

If attention is paid as to whether a vowel is long or short, no difficulty will present itself in placing the stress on the right syllable in a word of more than one syllable. When a word has two or three short syllables, all are pronounced equally short, and no stress is placed on any of them. When a double consonant occurs between two vowels, the first of the consonants is pronounced *after* the first vowel, but the second *before* the second vowel; e.g. كسّر *kassara* (*kas-sa-ra*), 'he broke to pieces.'

a short,	like the sound of		*a* in	hat
ā long	,,	,,	*a* ,,	father
i short	,,	,,	*i* ,,	bit
ī long	,,	,,	*i* ,,	machine
u short	,,	,,	*u* ,,	put
ū long	,,	,,	*u* ,,	rule
au diphthong	,,	,,	*ow* ,,	cow
ai ,,	,,	,,	*ai* ,,	aisle

VOCABULARIES.

[The Arabic language has only one definite article, ال *al*, 'the,' which has purposely been omitted in the Arabic column.]

The World and Nature.

ENGLISH.	ARABIC.	PRONUNCIATION.
air	هوا	hawa
autumn	خريف	kharīf
cloud	غيم	ghaim, *pl.* ghuyūm
cold	بَرْد	bard
darkness	ظلمه	ẓulmah
dew	ندَى	nada
earth	ارض	arḍ
earthquake	زلزله	zalzalah
east	شرق	sharq
eclipse of the sun	كسوف	kusūf
,, ,, moon	خسوف	khusūf
fire	نار	nār
fog, mist	ضباب	ḍabāb
frost	صقيع	ṣaqī'
hail	برد	barad
heat	حرّ	ḥarr
ice	جليد	jalīd
light	نور	nūr

Vowel sounds. hat, fāther, bit, machīne, put, rūle, aisle; au=ow in cow.
Dotted consonants, ḥ, ḍ, ṣ, ṭ, ẓ, **hard.**

English.	Arabic.	Pronunciation.
lightning	برق	barq
moon	قمر	qamar
nature	طبيعه	ṭabīʻah
north	شمال	shamāl
north-west	شمال غربى	shamāl gharbi
planet	كوكب	kaukab
rain	مطر	maṭar
rainbow	قوس قدح	qaus qadaḥ
shade	ظلّ	ẓill
shadow	فيء	fai
snow	ثلج	thalj
south	جنوب	junūb
spring	ربيع	rabīʻ
star	نجمه	nijmah
storm	نو	nau
summer	صيف	ṣaif
sun	شمس	shams
tempest	عاصفه	ʻāṣifah
thunder	رعد	raʻd
water	ماء - ميّه	mā - maiyah
weather	طقس	ṭaqs
fine weather	صحو	ṣaḥu
west	غرب	gharb
whirlwind	زوبعه	zaubaʻah
wind	ريح	rīḥ
winter	شتا	shita
world	دنيا - عالم	dunya, ʻālam

Vowel sounds: hat, fāther, bit, machīne, put, rūle, aisle; **au=ow** in c
Dotted consonants, ḥ, ḍ, ṣ, ṭ, ẓ, **hard**.

Land and Water.

English.	Arabic.	Pronunciation.
bank	شطّ	shaṭṭ
clay	طين	ṭīn
desert	صحراء	ṣaḥrā
field	حقل	ḥaql
forest	حرش	ḥarsh, *pl.* aḥrāsh
garden	بستان	bustān
gulf	خليج	khalīj
hill	تلّ	tall
island	جزيرة	jazīrah
lake	بحيرة	buḥairah
land	ارض	arḍ
meadow	مرج	marj
mountain	جبل	jabal
ocean	البحر المحيط	al-baḥr l-muḥīṭ
plain	سهل	sahl
port	مينا	mīna
river	نهر	nahr
rock	صخر	ṣakhr
sea	بحر	baḥr
shore	ساحل	sāḥil
spring	عين	'ain
valley	وادي	wādi
water, clear	ماء صافي	mā ṣāfi
,, cold	ماء بارد	mā bārid
,, hot	ما سخن	mā sukhun
wave	موج	mauj

Vowel sounds: **hat, fāther, bit, machīne, put, rūle, aisle; au = ow** in cow.
Dotted consonants, ḥ, ḍ, ṣ, ṭ, ẓ, **hard**.

Metals, Minerals, etc.

ENGLISH.	ARABIC.	PRONUNCIATION.
amber	كهربا	kahraba
arsenic	زرنيخ	zarnīkh
brass	نحاس اصفر	naḥās aṣfar
bronze	نحاس اسود	naḥās aswad
charcoal	فحم حطب	faḥm ḥaṭab
coal	فحم حجر	faḥm ḥajar
copper	نحاس احمر	naḥās aḥmar
diamond	الماس	almās
flint	صوّان	ṣawwān
glass	قزاز	qazāz
gold	ذهب	dhahab
iron	حديد	ḥadīd
lead	رصاص	raṣāṣ
marble	رخام	rukhām
metal	معدن	ma‘dan
mineral	معدنى	ma‘dani
pearl	لؤلؤه	lu'lu'ah
pebble	حصوه	ḥaṣwah
quicksilver	زيبق	zaibaq
sand	رمل	raml
silver	فضه	faḍḍah
steel	بولاد	būlād
stone	حجر	ḥajar
sulphur	كبريت	kibrīt
tin	تنك ـ قصدير	tanak, qaṣdīr
zinc	توتيا ـ زنك	tūtiya, zink

Vowel sounds : **hat, fāther, bit, machīne, put, rūle, aisle ; au = ow in**
Dotted consonants, **ḥ, ḍ, ṣ, ṭ, ẓ, hard.**

Animals and Birds.

ENGLISH.	ARABIC.	PRONUNCIATION.
animal	حيوان	ḥaiwān
bird	طير	ṭair
birdlime	دبق	dibq
calf	عجل	ʿijl
camel	جمل	jamal
hump of the camel	سنامه الجمل	sanāmat-l-jamal
cat	قطّه	quṭṭah
cattle	مواشى	mawāshi
chicken	فرخ	farkh, *pl.* afrākh
cock	ديک	dīk
cow	بقره	baqarah
crow	غراب	ghurāb
dog	کلب	kalb
donkey	حمار	ḥimār
dove	حمامه	ḥamāmah
dromedary	هجين	hajīn
duck	بطّه	baṭṭah
eagle	نسر	nisr
elephant	فيل	fīl
fox	ثعلب	thaʿlab
gazelle	غزال	ghazāl
goat	معزى	miʿza
goose	وزّه	wazzah
hare	ارنب	arnab
hawk	صقر	ṣaqr

Vowel sounds: **hat**, fāther, bit, machīne, **put**, rūle, **aisle**; **au = ow** in cow.
Dotted consonants, ḥ, ḍ, ṣ, ṭ, ẓ, **hard**.

English.	Arabic.	Pronunciation.
hen	دجاجه	dajājah
hide (of a beast)	جلد	jild
horn	قرن	qarn
horse	حصان	ḥiṣān
jackal	ابن آوى	ibn-āwa (*local* wā
lamb	خروف	kharūf
lark	قنبره	qunbarah
lion	اسد	asad
lioness	لبوه	labwah
mare	فرس	faras
monkey	سعدان	sa'dān
mouse	فار	fār
mule	بغل	baghl
owl	بومه	būmah
ox	ثور	thaur
parrot	ببغا	babaghā
partridge	حجل	ḥajal
pelican	رخم	rakham
pig	خنزير	khanzīr
pigeon	يمامه	yamāmah
quail	سمانى	sumāna
rat	جرذون	jirdhaun
sheep	غنم	ghanam
sparrow	عصفور	'aṣfūr
swallow	سنونو	sunūnu
turkey	دجاج هندي	dujāj hindi
wolf	ذئب	zi'b

Vowel sounds: hat, fāther, bit, machīne, put, rūle, aisle; **au=ow** in cow.
Dotted consonants, ḥ, ḍ, ṣ, ṭ, ẓ, **hard.**

Reptiles and Insects.

English.	Arabic.	Pronunciation.
ant	نمله	namlah
bee	نحله	naḥlah
bug	بقّه	baqqah
butterfly	فراشه	farāshah, *pl.* farāsh
crocodile	تمساح	timsāḥ
flea	برغوت	barghūt
fly	ذبّانه	dhubbānah
frog	ضفضعه	ḍufḍa'ah
gnat	برغشه	barghashah, *pl.* barghash
grasshopper	جندب	jundub
insect	حشره	ḥashrah, *pl.* hasharāt
locust	جراد	jarād
mosquito	ناموسه	nāmūsah, *pl.* nāmūs
moth	بعوضه	ba'ūḍah
reptiles	زحافات	zaḥḥāfāt
silkworm	دودة حرير	dūdat-ḥarīr
snail	حلزون	ḥalazaun
snake	حيّه	ḥaiyah
spider	عنكبوت	'ankabūt
sting	قرصه	qarṣah *or* las'ah
wasp	دبّور	dabbūr
worm	دوده	dūdah

Vowel sounds: hat, fāther, bit, machīne, put, rūle, aisle; **au = ow** in cow.
Dotted consonants, ḥ, ḍ, ṣ, ṭ, ẓ, **hard.**

Times and Seasons.

Days of the week:

English.	Arabic.	Pronunciation.
Sunday	الاحد	al-aḥad
Monday	الاثنين	al-ithnain
Tuesday	الثلاثا	al-thalāthā
Wednesday	الاربعا	al-arba'a
Thursday	الخميس	al-khamīs
Friday	الجمعه	al-jum'a
Saturday	السبت	al-sabt

Months of the year:

English.	Arabic.	Pronunciation.
January	كانون ثانى	kānūn thāni
February	شباط	shubāṭ
March	اذار	ādhār
April	نيسان	nīsān
May	ايّار	aiyār
June	حزيران	ḥuzairān
July	تمّوز	tammūz
August	آب	āb
September	ايلول	ailūl
October	تشرين اوّل	tishrīn awwal
November	تشرين ثانى	tishrīn thāni
December	كانون اوّل	kānūn awwal

Mohammedan names of the months:

المحرّم	Al-Muḥarram	جمادى الاولى	Jumādā-l-ūla
صفر	Ṣafar	جمادى الاخره	Jumādā-l-ākhirah
ربيع الاوّل	Rabī'-l-awwal		
ربيع الثانى	Rabī'-l-thāni	رجب	Rajab

Vowel sounds: hat, fāther, bit, machīne, put, rūle, aisle; **au** = **ow** in cow.
Dotted consonants, ḥ, ḍ, ṣ, ṭ, ẓ, **hard.**

شعبان	Sha'bān	شوّال	Shauwāl
رمضان	Ramaḍān (the month of fasting)	ذوالقعده	Dhulqa'dah
		ذوالحجّه	Dhulḥijjah

The Mohammedans count according to lunar years of 354 days, so that thirty-four lunar years are equal to about thirty-three solar. Their first year began on July 16, 622 A.D.

ENGLISH.	ARABIC.	PRONUNCIATION.
afternoon	عصر	'aṣr
age, an	قرن - جيل	qarn, jīl
beginning, the	الابتدآء	al-ibtidā
daily	يوميّ	yaumī
day	يوم	yaum, *pl.* aiyām
daybreak	طلوع النهار	ṭulū'-l-nahār
daytime	نهار	nahār
day after to-morrow	بعد غد	ba'd ghad
,, before yesterday	اول امس	awwal ams
every day	كلّ يوم	kull yaum
dawn	الفجر	al-fajr
early	باكر - بدري	bākir, badrī
end, the	الانتهآء	al-intihā
evening (early)	مغرب	maghrib
,, (late)	عشآء - مسآء	'ishā, masa
full moon	بدر	badr
hour	ساعه	sa'ah, *pl.* sa'āt
half an hour	نصف ساعه	nisf sā'ah
leap year	سنة كبيس	sanat kabīs
lunar months	شهور قمريّه	shuhūr qamariyah
midday, noon	الظهر	al-ẓuhr
middle, the	الوسط	al-wasaṭ

Vowel sounds: hat, fāther, bit, machīne, put, rūle, aisle; au = ow in cow. *Dotted consonants,* ḥ, ḍ, ṣ, ṭ, ẓ, hard.

English.	Arabic.	Pronunciation.
midnight	نصف الليل	nișfu-l-lail
minute	دقيقه	daqīqah
month	شهر	shahr, *pl.* shuhūr
morning	الصباح	al-șabāh
night	الليل	al-lail
season	فصل	fașl
seasons, the	الفصول	al-fușūl
spring	ربيع	rabī'
summer	صيف	șaif
autumn	خريف	kharīf
winter	شتا	shita
sunrise	طلوع الشمس	țulū'-l-shams
sunset	غروب الشمس	ghurūb-l-shams
time	وقت	waqt
to-day	اليوم	al-yaum
to-morrow	غدا	ghada
to-morrow morning	غدا صباحًا	ghada șabāḥan
week	جمعه - اسبوع	jum'ah, usbū'
two weeks	جمعتين	jum'atain
year	سنه	sanah, *pl.* sinīn
yesterday	امس	ams

Mankind ; Relations.

age	عمر	'umr
old age	شيخوخه	shaikhūkhah
aunt (maternal)	خاله	khālah

Vowel sounds: hat, fāther, bit, machīne, put, rūle, aisle; **au**=**ow** in cow.
Dotted consonants, ḥ, ḍ, ṣ, ṭ, ẓ, **hard.**

ENGLISH.	ARABIC.	PRONUNCIATION.
aunt (paternal)	عمّه	ʻammah
bachelor, spinster	عزب	ʻazab
boy	صبيّ	ṣabi
bride	عروس	ʻarūs
bridegroom	عريس	ʻarīs
brother	اخ	akh
child	ولد	walad
cousin (masc.)	ابن العمّ - ابن الخال	ibn-l-ʻamm, ibn-l-khāl
,, (fem.)	ابنة العمّ - ابنة الخال	ibnat-l-ʻamm, ibnat-l-khāl
daughter	ابنه	ibnah
father	اب	āb
female	انثى	untha
girl	بنت	bint
grandfather	جدّ	jidd
grandmother	جدّه	jiddah
grandson	حفيد	ḥafīd
granddaughter	حفيده	ḥafīdah
husband	زوج	zauj
infancy	طفوليّه	ṭufūliya
madam (Mrs.)	ست	sit
maiden (virgin)	بكر	bikr
male	ذكر	dhakar
man	رجل	rajul, *pl.* rijāl
mother	امّ	umm
negro	عبد	ʻabd, *fem.* ʻabdah

Vowel sounds: hat, fāther, bit, machīne, put, rūle, aisle; au = ow in cow. *Dotted consonants*, ḥ, ḍ, ṣ, ṭ, ẓ, hard.

English.	Arabic.	Pronunciation.
nephew	ابن الاخ - ابن الاخت	ibn-l-akh, ibn-l-ukht
niece	ابنة الاخ - ابنة الاخت	ibnat-l-akh, ibnat-l-ukht
orphan	يتيم	yatīm, *fem.* yatīmah
parents	والدين	wālidain
people	ناس	nās, *sing.* insān
relation	قرابه	qarābah
relative	قريب	qarīb
servant	خادم	khādim, *fem.* khādimah
sir (Mr.)	سيّد	saiyid
sister	اخت	ukht
slave (female)	جاريه	jāriyah
son	ابن	ibn
uncle (maternal)	خال	khāl
„ (paternal)	عمّ	ʻamm
widow	ارمله	armalah
widower	ارمل	armal
wife	زوجه	zaujah
woman	امرأه	imraʼāh
youth	شباب	shabāb
youth, a	شبّ	shabb

The Human Body.

ankle	كعب	kaʻb
arm	ذراع	dhirāʻ
back	ظهر	ẓahr

Vowel sounds: hat, fāther, bit, machīne, put, rūle, aisle; au = ow in cow
Dotted consonants, ḥ, ḍ, ṣ, ṭ, ẓ, hard.

English.	Arabic.	Pronunciation.
beard	لحيه	liḥyah
belly	بطن	baṭn, *pl.* buṭūn
blood	دمّ	damm
body	جسد	jasad
bowels	امعآء	am'ā
brain	دماغ	dimāgh
breath	نفس	nafas
cheek	خدّ	khadd, *pl.* khudūd
chest	صدر	ṣadr, *pl.* ṣudūr
chin	ذقن	dhaqn, *pl.* dhuqūn
ear	اذن	udhn, *pl.* ādhān
elbow	كوع	kū', *pl.* akwā'
eye	عين	'ain
eyebrows	حاجب	ḥājib
eyelash	رمش	rimsh
eyelid	جفن	jifn
face	وجه	wajh
finger	اصبع	iṣba', *pl.* aṣābi'
foot	رجل	rijl, *pl.* arjul
forehead	جبين	jibīn
hair	شعر	sha'r
hand	يد	yad
left hand	شمال	shimāl
right hand	يمين	yamīn
head	راس	rās
heart	قلب	qalb
heel	عقب	'aqab

ENGLISH.	ARABIC.	PRONUNCIATION.
kidneys	كليه	kilyah
knee	ركبه	rukbah, *pl.* rukab
leg	ساق	sāq
lip	شفه	shiffah
liver	كبد	kabid
lungs	رئه	rī'ah
molar	درس	dirs
moustache	شارب	shārib
mouth	فم	fam
muscle	عضله	'aḍalah
nail	ظفر	ẓifr, *pl.* aẓafīr
navel	سرّه	surrah
neck	رقبه	raqabah
nerve	عصب	'aṣab
nose	انف	anf
palm of the hand	كفّ	kaff
shoulder	كتف	katif, *pl.* aktāf
skin	جلد	jild
spine	سلسلة الظهر	silsilat-l-ẓahr
stomach	معده	mi'dah
temple	صدغ	ṣudgh
throat	حلق	ḥalq
thumb	باهم	bāhim
tongue	لسان	lisān
tooth	سنّ	sinn
vein	عرق	'irq, *pl.* 'urūq
wrist	معصم	mi'ṣam

Vowel sounds: hat, fāther, bit, machīne, put, rūle, aisle; **au = ow** in co
Dotted consonants, ḥ, ḍ, ṣ, ṭ, ẓ, **hard.**

Physical and Mental Powers, Qualities, etc.

English	Arabic.	Pronunciation.
anger	غضب	ghaḍab
character	خلق	khulq, *pl.* akhlāq
confidence	ثقه	thiqah
courage	شجاعه	shajā'ah
desire	رغبه	rughbah
despair	يأس ـ قنوط	ya's, qunūṭ
emotions	انفعال نفسانى	infi'āl nafsāni
envy	حسد	ḥasad
exercise	رياضه	riyāḍah
experience	خبرة	khibrah
fear, reverence	تقوى	taqwah
folly	جنون	junūn
forgetfulness	نسيان	nisyān
fright	خوف	khauf
goodness	صلاح	ṣalāḥ
grief	غمّ	ghamm
hatred	بغضة	bughḍah
honesty	امانه	amānah
honour	اكرام	ikrām
hope	امل ـ رجاء	amal, raja
intelligence	فهم	fahm
joy	فرح	faraḥ
judgment (opinion)	راي	rāi
justice	عدل	'adl
kindness	معروف	ma'rūf

Vowel sounds: hat, fāther, bit, machīne, put, rūle, aisle; au = ow in cow.
Dotted consonants, ḥ, ḍ, ṣ, ṭ, ẓ, hard.

English.	Arabic.	Pronunciation.
laughter	ضحك	ḍiḥk
love	محبّة	maḥabbah
memory	ذاكره	dhākirah
mercy	رحمه	raḥmah
modesty	احتشام	iḥtishām
pain	وجع	waja'
patience	صبر	ṣabr
piety	تديّن	tadaiyun
pleasure	سرور	surūr
politeness	ادب	adab
pride	كبرياء	kubriyā
prudence	بصيره	baṣīrah
reason	عقل	'aql
senses, the	الحواس	al-ḥawās
feeling, touch	اللمس	al-lams
hearing	السمع	al-sama'
seeing, sight	النظر	al-naẓar
smelling, smell	الشمّ	al-shamm
tasting, taste	الذوق	al-dhauq
shame	عيب - خجل	'aib, khajal
smile	ابتسام	ibtisām
sneeze	عطسه	'aṭsah
sorrow	حزن	ḥuzn
soul	نفس	nafs
speech	كلام	kalām
spirit	روح	rūḥ
strength	قوّه	quwwah

English.	Arabic.	Pronunciation.
stupidity	غباوه	ghabāwah
surprise	انذهال	indhihāl
suspicion	شبهه	shubhah
thought	فكر	fikr
voice	صوت	ṣaut
will	اراده	irādah
wisdom	حكمه	ḥikmah

Diseases of the Body.

ague	دوريّه	dauriyah
apoplexy	فالج	fālij
asthma	ضيق النفس	ḍīq-l-nafaṣ
biliousness	صفراء	ṣafra
blind	اعمى	a'ma
bruise	رضّ	raḍḍ
burn	حرق	ḥarq
cholera	هوا اصفر	hawa aṣfar
cold, a	رشح - نزله	rashḥ, nazlah
colic	مغص	maghṣ
consumption	السلّ	al-sall
contagion	عدوى	'adwa
cough	سعال	su'āl
deaf	اطرش	aṭrash
death	موت	maut
diarrhœa	اسهال	ishāl
dumb	اخرس	akhras
dysentery	زحير - دوسنطاريا	zaḥīr, dusunṭāriya

Vowel sounds: **bat, fāther, bit, machīne, put, rūle, aisle; au = ow in cow.**
Dotted consonants, **ḥ, ḍ, ṣ, ṭ, ẓ, hard.**

English.	Arabic.	Pronunciation.
faintness	اغماء	ighmā
fever	سخونه	sukhūnah
fracture	كسر	kasr
gout	نقرس	niqris
headache	وجع راس	wajaʻ rās
indigestion	سوء الهضم	sū'-l-haḍm
inflammation	التهاب	iltihāb
illness	مرض	maraḍ
jaundice	يرقان	yaraqān
lame	اعرج	aʻraj
measles	حصبه	ḥaṣbah
plague	طاعون	ṭāʻūn
smallpox	جدري	jadari
sore throat	وجع الحلق	wajaʻ-l-ḥalq
toothache	وجع السنّ	wajaʻ-l-sinn
wound	جرح	jurḥ, *pl.* jurūḥ

Dress.

apron	مريول	maryūl
boot	جزمه	jazmah
button	زرّ	zirr, *pl.* azrār
cap	طربوش	ṭarbūsh
cloth (cotton)	خام	khām
,, (wool)	جوخ	jūkh
coat	جبّه	jubbah
collar	ياقه	yāqah
collar of coat, etc.	قبّه	qabbah

Vowel sounds: hat, fāther, bit, maçhīne, put, rūle, aisle; au = ow in co[w]
Dotted consonants, ḥ, ḍ, ṣ, ṭ, ẓ, hard.

English.	Arabic.	Pronunciation.
comb	مشط	musht
cotton	قطن	quṭun
drawers	سروال	sirwāl
frock	فسطان	fusṭān
gloves	كفوف	kufūf
gown	قفطان	qafṭān
handkerchief	منديل	mandīl
hat	برنيطه	burnaiṭah
lace	دانتله	dāntellah
linen	ثياب بيض	thiyāb bīḍ
mantle	عباءه	'abāh
muslin	شاش	shāsh
needle	ابره	ibrah
petticoat	تنوره	tannūrah
pin	دبّوس	dabbūs
purse	كيس	kīs
razor	موس	mūs
ring	خاتم	khātim
scissors	مقصّ	miqaṣṣ
serviette	فوطه	fūṭah
shawl	شال	shāl
sheet	شرشف	sharshaf
shirt	قميص	qamīṣ
shoe	مداس	madās
silk	حرير	ḥarīr
sleeve	كُمّ	kumm
slippers	بابوج	babūj

Vowel sounds: hat, fāther, bit, machīne, put, rūle, aisle; au = ow in cow.
Dotted consonants, ḥ, ḍ, ṣ, ṭ, ẓ, hard.

English.	Arabic.	Pronunciation.
soap	صابون	ṣābūn
spectacles	نظّارة العيون	naẓẓārat-l-ʻuyūn
sponge	سفاجه	safinjah
stockings	شرابات	sharābāt
suit of clothes	بدله	badlah
thimble	كشتبان	kushtubān
thread	غزل	ghazl
trousers (Arab)	شروال	shirwāl
,, (pair of)	بنطلون	banṭalūn
umbrella	شمسيّه	shamsiyah
veil	برقع	burquʻ
waistcoat	صدريّه	ṣadriyah
watch	ساعه	sāʻah

House and Furniture.

English.	Arabic.	Pronunciation.
basin	طست	ṭast
basket	سلّه	sallah
bath	حمّام	ḥammām
bed	فراش	firāsh
bedstead	تخت	takht
bell	جرس	jaras
blanket	حرام	ḥirām
bottle	قنينه	qannīnah
broom	مكنسه	miknasah
brush	فرشه	furshah
candle	شمعه	shamʻah
candlestick	شمعدان	shamʻadān

ENGLISH	ARABIC.	PRONUNCIATION.
carpet	سجّادة	sujjādah
,, (large)	بساط	bisāṭ
chair	كرسى	kursi
chest of drawers	جارور	jārūr
chimney	مدخنه	madkhanah
cupboard	خزانه	khazānah
curtain	ستارة	sitārah
cushion	مخدّة	mikhaddah
door	باب	bāb
floor	ارضيّه	arḍiyah
furniture	آثاث	āthāth
garden	بستان	bustān
holy well (at Mekka)	زمزم	zamzam
house	بيت	bait
house to let	بيت للايجار	bait-lil-ījār
jug	كوز	kūz
key	مفتاح	miftāḥ
kitchen	مطبخ	maṭbakh
landlord	مؤجّر	mu'ajjir
lease	ايجار	ījār
lock	قفل	qifl
looking-glass	مرايه	mirayah
mat	حصيرة	ḥaṣīrah
matches	كبريت	kibrīt
mattress	طرّاحه	ṭarrāḥah
pail	سطل	saṭl
picture	تصويرة	taṣwīrah

Vowel sounds: hat, fāther, bit, machīne, put, rūle, aisle; au = ow in cow
Dotted consonants, ḥ, ḍ, ṣ, ṭ, ẓ, hard.

English.	Arabic.	Pronunciation.
quilt	لحاف	liḥāf
roof	سقف	saqf
room	اوضه	auḍah
sofa	ديوان	diwān
stable	اسطبل	isṭabl
staircase	درج	daraj
table	سفره	sufrah
tenant	مستأجر	mustā'jir
towel	بشكير	bashkīr
wall	حايط	ḥāyiṭ
wardrobe	خزانة ثياب	khazānat thiyāb
water-closet	مستراح	mustarāḥ
well	بير	bīr
window	شبّاك	shubbāk

Food, Drink, and Smoking.

(For Conversations, see p. 116.)

appetite	شهيّة	shahiyah
beef	لحم بقر	laḥm baqar
beer	بيرا	bīra
biscuits	بقسماط	buqsumāṭ
bouillon, broth	مرقة لحم	maraqat laḥm
brandy	كنياك	kunyāk
bread	خبز	khubz
breakfast	فطور	faṭūr
butter	زبده	zibdah
cake	كعك	kak

Vowel sounds: hat, fāther, bit, machīne, put, rūle, aisle; **au = ow in cow.**
Dotted consonants, ḥ, ḍ, ṣ, ṭ, ẓ, **hard.**

English.	Arabic.	Pronunciation.
cheese	جبنه	jibnah
chicken	فرخ	farkh
chocolate	شوكولاته	shukulātah
coffee	قهوه	qahwah
cooked	مطبوخ	maṭbūkh
cream	قشطه	qashṭah
dessert	نقل	nuql
dinner	غدا	ghada
dish	صحن كبير	ṣaḥn kabīr
egg	بيضه	baiḍah
eggs (boiled)	بيض مسلوق	baiḍ maslūq
,, (fried)	بيض مقلى	baiḍ maqli
fat	دهن	dihn
fish	سمك	samak
flour	طحين	ṭaḥīn
food	قوت	qūt
fork	شوكه	shaukah
glass of water	كبّاية ماء	kubbayat mā
glass of wine	قدح نبيذ	qadaḥ nabīdh
honey	عسل	'asal
hunger	جوع	jū'
ice	جليد - ثلج	jalīd, thalj
jam	مربّى	murabba
knife	سكّينه	sikkīnah
lamb	لحم خروف	laḥm kharūf
lemonade	لاموناده	lamunāduh
liquor	عرق	'arak

Vowel sounds: hat, fāther, bit, machīne, put, rūle, aisle; **au** = **ow** in cow.
Dotted consonants, ḥ, ḍ, ṣ, ṭ, ẓ, **hard.**

ENGLISH.	ARABIC.	PRONUNCIATION.
meat	لحم	laḥm
,, (roast)	لحم مسلوق	laḥm maslūq
,, (boiled)	لحم مشوي	laḥm mashwi
milk	حليب	ḥalīb
sour milk	لبن	laban
mouthful, a	لقمه	luqmah
mustard	خردل	khardal
mutton	لحم غنم	laḥm ghanam
napkin	فوطه	fūṭah
oil	زيت	zait
omelet	عجة بيض	'ijjat baiḍ
pepper	فلفل	filfil
pie	رقاق ـ فطير محشوّ	riqāq, faṭīr maḥshu
plate	صحن	ṣaḥn
pork	لحم خنزير	laḥm khanzīr
salad	سلطه	salaṭah
salt	ملح	milḥ
sauce	مرقه	maraqah
smoking	تدخين	tadkhīn
cigar *or* cigarette	سيكاره	sikārah
pipe	غليون	ghalyūn
tobacco	تبغ ـ دخّان	tabagh, dukhkhān
tobacco pouch	كيس دخّان	kīs dukhkhān
soup	شوربا	shauraba
spoon	معلقه	ma'laqah
sugar	سكّر	sukkar

English.	Arabic.	Pronunciation.
sugar and water	ماء سكّر	mā sukkar
supper	عشا	'asha
sweets	حلويّات	ḥalawiyāt
tea	شاي	shāi
thirst	عطش	'aṭash
tongue	لسان	lisān
veal	لحم عجل	laḥm 'ijl
vinegar	خلّ	khall
water	ماء	mā
wine	نبيذ	nabīdh

Vegetables.

artichoke	خرشوف	kharshūf
asparagus	هليون	halyūn
barley	شعير	sha'īr
beans	فول	fūl
cabbage	ملفوف	malfūf
caper	قبّار	qabbār
carrot	جزر	jazar
cauliflower	قرنبيط	qarnabīṭ
celery	كرفس	karafs
cinnamon	قرفه	qirfah
corn	حبوب - غلّه	ḥubūb, ghallah
cress	رشاد	rashād
cucumbers	خيار	khiyār
flour	طحين	ṭaḥīn
garlic	توم	tūm

Vowel sounds: hat, fāther, bit, machīne, put, rūle, aisle; au = ow in cow.
Dotted consonants, ḥ, ḍ, ṣ, ṭ, ẓ, **hard.**

English.	Arabic.	Pronunciation.
gourd	قرع	qar'
grass	حشيش	ḥashīsh
hay	حشيش ناشف	ḥashīsh nāshif
herb	بقل	baql
leek	كرّات	kurrāt
lentils	عدس	'adas
lettuce	خسّ	khass
maize	ذره	dhurah
mushroom	فطر	fuṭr
oats	هرطم	hurṭum
olives	زيتون	zaitūn
onion	بصل	baṣal
parsley	بقدونس	baqdūnis
peas	بزلّه - حمّص	bizillah, hummuṣ
potatoes	بطاطا	baṭaṭa
radishes	فجل	fijl
rice	رزّ	ruzz
spinach	سبانخ	sabānikh
straw	قشّ	qashsh
tomatoes	بندوره	bandūrah
turnip	لفت	lift
vegetables	خضره	khuḍrah

Fruits.

almonds	لوز	lauz
apples	تفّاح	tuffāḥ
apricots	مشمش	mishmish

ENGLISH.	ARABIC.	PRONUNCIATION
cherries	قراصيا	qarāṣya
chestnuts	كستنه	kastanah
currants	عنب الثعلب	ʻinab-l-thaʻlab
dates	بلح	balaḥ
figs	تين	tīn
fruits	فواكه	fawākih
gooseberries	ثمر افرنجي	thamar ifranji
grapes	عنب	ʻinab
lemons	ليمون	laimūn
medlars	زعرور	zaʻrūr
melons	بطّيخ	baṭṭīkh
mulberries	توت	tūt
nuts	بندق	bunduq
oranges	بردقان	burdaqān
peaches	درّاق	durrāq
pears	انجاص	injāṣ
plums	خوخ	khaukh
pomegranates	رمّان	rummān
raisins	زبيب	zabīb
raspberries	ثمر العلّيق	thamar-l-ʻullaiq
strawberries	فروله	faraulah
walnuts	جوز	jauz

Town, Country, and Agriculture.

bath	حمّام	ḥammām
bridge	جسر	jisr
building	بنيان	bunyān

Vowel sounds: hat, fāther, bit, machīne, put, rūle, aisle; au = ow in cow.
Dotted consonants, ḥ, ḍ, ṣ, ṭ, ẓ, hard.

ENGLISH.	ARABIC.	PRONUNCIATION.
cemetery	مقبره	maqbarah
church	كنيسه	kanīsah
citadel	قلعه	qal'ah
coffee-house	قهوه	qahwah
consulate	قونسلاتو	qunslātu
court of justice	محكمه	maḥkamah
courtyard	حوش	ḥaush
custom-house	بيت الكمرك	bait-l-kumruk
desert	بريه	barriyah
embassy	سفاره	safārah
farm	مزرعه	mazra'ah
farmer	فلاّح	fallāḥ
fence	سياج	siyāj
flock	قطيع	qaṭī'
fountain, spring	حوض	ḥauḍ
gate	بوّابه	bauwabah
harvest	حصاد	ḥaṣād
horse fair	سوق الخيل	sūq-l-khail
hospital	سبيتال	sbitāl
hotel	لوكانده	lūkāndah
labourer	فاعل	fā'il
lane	زقاق	zuqāq
library	كتبخانه	kutubkhānah
manure	زبل	zibl
market	سوق	sūq
fish-market	سوق السّمك	sūq-l-samak
meadow	مرج	marj

Vowel sounds: hat, fāther, bit, machīne, put, rūle, aisle; **au = ow** in cow.
Dotted consonants, ḥ, ḍ, ṣ, ṭ, ẓ, **hard.**

English.	Arabic.	Pronunciation.
mile	ميل	mīl
mill	طاحونه	ṭāḥūnah
mosque	جامع	jāmi'
palace	سرايه - قصر	sarāyah, qaṣr
pasture	مرعى	mar'a
plough	محراث	miḥrāth
police-office	ضابطيّه	ẓābtiyah
pond	بركه	birkah
post-office	محلّ البوسطه	maḥall-l-bōstah
prison	حبس	ḥabs
promenade	محلّ نزهه	maḥall nuzhah
quarter (of town)	حاره	ḥārah
railway	سكّة حديد	sikkat ḥadīd
river	نهر	nahr
road	طريق	ṭarīq
school	مدرسه	madrasah
seed	بزر	bizr
sheaf	حزمه	ḥuzmah
sheep fair	سوق الغنم	sūq-l-ghanam
shepherd	راعى	rā'i
shop	دكّان	dukkān
spring	عين	'ain
square	ميدان	mīdān
station	محطّه	maḥaṭ ah
street	شارع	shāri'
tavern	خمّاره	khammārah
tower	برج	burj

Vowel sounds: hat, fāther, bit, machīne, put, rūle, aisle; **au = ow in cow.**
Dotted consonants, ḥ, ḍ, ṣ, ṭ, ẓ, **hard.**

ENGLISH.	ARABIC.	PRONUNCIATION.
town	مدينه	madīnah
valley	وادي	wādi
village	قريه	karyah
wood, forest	حرش	ḥursh

Professions and Trades.

ambassador	سفير	safīr
architect	مهندس	muhandis
auctioneer	دلّال	dallāl
baker	خبّاز	khabbāz
barber	حلّاق	ḥallāq
blacksmith	حدّاد	ḥaddād
bookbinder	مجلّد كتب	mujallid kutb
bookseller	كتبي	kutbī
carpenter	نجّار	najjār
chemist	كيماوي	kimāwi
clergyman	قسّيس	qassīs
clerk	كاتب	kātib
coachman	عربجي	ʻarbaji
consul	قنصل	qunṣul
contractor	مقاول	muqāwil
doctor	طبيب - حكيم	ṭabīb, ḥakīm
dragoman	ترجمان	turjumān
goldsmith	صايغ	ṣayigh
governor	حاكم	ḥākim
grocer	بقّال	baqqāl
groom	سايس - مكاري	sāyis, mukāri

Vowel sounds: hat, fāther, bit, machīne, put, rūle, aisle; au = ow in
Dotted consonants, ḥ, ḍ, ṣ, ṭ, ẓ, hard.

English.	Arabic.	Pronunciation.
guide	دليل	dalīl
interpreter	ترجمان	turjumān
jeweller	جواهرجى	jawāhirji
judge	قاضى	qāḍi
laundress	غسّاله	ghassālah
lawyer	محامى	muḥāmi
locksmith	قفّال	qaffāl
merchant	تاجر	tājir
midwife	دايه	dāyah
missionary	مرسل	mursal
monk	راهب	rāhib
nun	راهبه	rāhibah
nurse	ممرّضه	mumarriḍah
oculist	حكيم عيون	ḥakīm ʻuyūn
officer	ظابط	ẓābiṭ
painter	مصوّر	muṣauwir
pharmacist	صيدلى	ṣaidali
policeman	بوليس	bolīs
porter	حمّال	ḥammāl
postman	بوسطجى	bostajī
postmaster	وكيل البوسطه	wakīl-l bōstah
preacher	واعظ	wāʻiẓ
printer	طبّاع	ṭabbāʻ
professor	استاذ	ustādh
sailor	بحريّ	baḥri
scholar	تلميذ	tilmīdh
sculptor	نقّاش	naqqāsh

Vowel sounds: hat, fāther, bit, machīne, put, rūle, **aisle**; **au**=**ow** in cow.
Dotted consonants, ḥ, ḍ, ṣ, ṭ, ẓ, **hard**.

ENGLISH.	ARABIC.	PRONUNCIATION.
servant	خدام	khaddām
shoemaker	سكّاف	sakkāf
soldier	عسكري	ʻaskari
surgeon	جرّاح	jarrāḥ
tailor	خيّاط	khaiyāṭ
teacher	معّلم	muʻallim
watchmaker	ساعاتى	saʻāti
watchman	غفير	ghafīr

Countries, Cities, and Nations.

Aleppo	حلب	ḥalab
Alexandria	اسكندريّه	iskandarīyah
America	اميركا	amirika
Arab, an	عربي	ʻarabi, *pl.* ʻurbān
Arabia	عربستان	ʻarabistān
Armenian, an	ارمني	armani
Asia	اسيا	asiya
Austria	النمسا	al-namsa
Austrian, an	نمساوي	namsāwi
Cairo	القاهره	al-qāhirah
China	الصين	al-ṣīn
Constantinople	اسطمبول	istambūl
Damascus	دمشق	dimashq
Egypt	مصر	miṣr
Egyptian, an	مصري	miṣri
England	بلاد الانكليز	bilād-l-inglīz
Englishman	انكليزي	inglīzi

ENGLISH.	ARABIC.	PRONUNCIATION.
Europe	اوربّا	ūrobba
France	فرانسا	farānsa
Frenchman	فرنساوي	faransāwi
German, a	المانى	almāni
Germany	المانيا	almāniya
Greece	بلاد الروم	bilād-l-rūm
Greek, a	رومي	rūmi
India	الهند	al-hind
Italian, an	ايطالياني	ītāliyāni
Italy	ايطاليا	ītāliya
Jerusalem	القدس	al-kuds
Jew	يهودي	yahūdi, *pl.* yahūd
Jordan, the	الاردن	al-ʻurdun
London	لندرا	londra
Paris	باريس	bārīs
Persia	بلاد العجم	bilād-l-ʻajam
Persian, a	عجمي	ʻajami
Rome	روميه	rūmiyah
Russia	بلاد المسكوب	bilād-l-maskōb
Russian, a	مسكوبي	maskōbi
Smyrna	ازمير	izmīr
Spain	اسبانيا	isbāniya
Spaniard	اسبانيولي	isbāniyōli
Syria	سوريّا	sūrīya
Turk	تركي	turki
Turkey	بلاد الترك	bilād-l-turk
Venice	بندقيّه	bunduqīyah

Vowel sounds: hat, fāther, bit, machīne, put, rūle, aisle; au = ow in cow.
Dotted consonants, ḥ, ḍ, ṣ, ṭ, ẓ, hard.

Travelling.

English.	Arabic.	Pronunciation.
arrival	وصول	wusūl
bridle	لجام	lijām
camel	ابل - جمل	ibl, jamal
,, driver	جمّال	jammāl
,, saddle	رحل	raḥl
caravan	قافله	qāfilah
carpet	بساط	bisāṭ
carriage	عربيّه	ʻarabīyah
donkey	حمار	ḥimār
donkey-driver	حمّار	ḥammār
excursion	سياحه قصيره	siyāḥa qaṣīrah
expenses	مصروف	masrūf
fowling-piece	باروده	bārūdah
girth	حزام - زنّار	hizām, zunnār
halter	رسن	rasan
highway	الدرب السلطاني	al-darb-l-sulṭāni
horse	حصان - فرس	hiṣān, faras
horseshoe	حذاء	ḥidhā
luggage	عفش	ʻafsh
money	دراهم	darāhim
to change money	صرف دراهم	sarf darāhim
mule	بغل	baghl
muleteer	مكاري	mukāri
Napoleon (20 fr. piece)	ليره فرنساويّه	līrah faransawīyah
package	حزمه	ḥuzmah

Vowel sounds: hat, fāther, bit, machīne, put, rūle, aisle; **au = ow** in cow.
Dotted consonants, ḥ, ḍ, ṣ, ṭ, ẓ, **hard.**

English.	Arabic.	Pronunciation.
passport	تذكره - بزبورت	tadhkara, bazabort
pistol	طبنجه	ṭabanjah
pound (£1)	ليره انكليزيّه	līrah inglizīyah
pound (Turkish)	ليره عثمانيّه	līrah ʻuthmānīyah
rope	حبل	ḥabl
saddle	سرج	sarj
spur	مهماز	mihmāz
stirrup	ركاب	rikāb
strap	سير	sair
tent	خيمه	khaimah
ticket	تذكره	tadhkara
tourist	سايح	sāyiḥ, *pl.* sīyāḥ
travel	سفر	safar
traveller	مسافر	musāfir
wages	اجره	ujrah
water-bottle	قربه	qirbah
water-jar	ابريق	ibrīq
whip	كرباج	kurbāj

Writing.

(For Conversations, see p. 118.)

address	عنوان	ʻinwān
blotting-paper	ورق نشاف	waraq nashshāf
book	كتاب	kitāb
compass	بيكار	bikār
date	تاريخ	tarīkh
dictionary	قاموس	qāmūs

Vowel sounds: hat, fāther, bit, machīne, put, rūle, aisle; au = ow in cow. *Dotted consonants*, ḥ, ḍ, ṣ, ṭ, ẓ, hard.

English.	Arabic.	Pronunciation
envelope	زرف	zarf
index (of a book)	فهرسه	fahrasah
ink	حبر	ḥibr
inkstand	دوايه	dawāyah
letter	مكتوب	maktūb
manuscript	كتاب خطّ	kitāb khaṭ
paper	ورق	waraq
sheet of paper	فرخ ورق	farkh waraq
pen	قلم - ريشه	qalam, rīshah
pencil	قلم رصاص	qalam ruṣāṣ
penknife	سكين	sikkīn
postage stamp	ورق دمغه	waraq damgha
registered (letter)	مسوكر	musaukar
ruler	مسطره	masṭarah
seal	ختم	khatm
sealing-wax	شمع احمر	sham' aḥmar
signature	امضاء	imḍa
writing	كتابه	kitābah

Colours.

(For Shopping, see p. 120.)

English.	Arabic.	Pronunciation
black	اسود	aswad
blue	ازرق	azraq
brown	اسمر	asmar
crimson	قرمزي	qirmizi
dark	قاتم - غامض	qātim, ghāmiḍ.
green	اخضر	akhḍar

Vowel sounds: **hat, fāther, bit, machīne, put, rūle, aisle; au = ow in cow.**
Dotted consonants, **ḥ, ḍ, ṣ, ṭ, ẓ, hard.**

ENGLISH.	ARABIC.	PRONUNCIATION.
greenish	خضراوي	khaḍrawi
grey	اشهب - رمادي	ashhab, ramādi
indigo	نيله	nīlah
light	فاتح	fātiḥ
orange	برتقاني	burtuqāni
pale	باهت	bāhit
pink	وردي خفيف	wardi khafīf
purple	ارجواني	urjuwāni
red	احمر	aḥmar
scarlet	قرمزي	qirmizi
sky-blue	سماوي	samāwi
violet	بنفسجي	banafsaji
white	ابيض	abyaḍ
yellow	اصفر	aṣfar
yellowish	مصفرّ	muṣfarr

Religious Terms.

angel	ملاك	malāk
apostle	رسول	rasūl
baptism	معموديّه	ma'mūdiyah
believer	مؤمن	mu'min
Bible	توراة	Taurāh
bishop	مطران	mutrān
Christian	مسيحي - نصراني	Masīḥi, Nuṣrāni
church	كنيسه	kanīsah
clergyman	قسّيس	qassīs
Creator	خالق	Khāliq

Vowel sounds: hat, fāther, bit, machīne, put, rūle, aisle; **au** = **ow** in cow.
- *Dotted consonants*, ḥ, ḍ, ṣ, ṭ, ẓ, **hard**.

ENGLISH.	ARABIC.	PRONUNCIATION.
devil	شيطان	shaiṭān
faith	أيمان	īmān
forgiveness	غفران	ghufrān
God	اللـه	Allāh
gospel	انجيل	injīl
heaven	سما	sama
hell	جهنّم	jahannam
Jesus Christ	يسوع المسيح	Yasū' el-Masīḥ
judgment	دينونه	dainūnah
Mohammedan	مسلم	Muslim
paradise	فردوس	firdaus
prayer	صلاه	ṣalāh
religion	دين	dīn
repentance	توبه	taubah
salvation	خلاص	khalāṣ
Saviour	مخلّص	Mukhalliṣ
spirit	روح	rūḥ

Adjectives.

ENGLISH.	ARABIC.	PRONUNCIATION.
able (capable)	قادر	qādir
amiable	محبوب	maḥbūb
angry	غضبان	ghaḍbān
ashamed	خجلان	khajlān
astonished	متحيّر	mutḥaiyir
bad	ردي	radi
barbarous	بربري	barbari
beautiful	جميل	jamīl

Vowel sounds: hat, fāther, bit, machīne, put, rūle, aisle; au = ow in cow.
Dotted consonants, ḥ, ḍ, ṣ, ṭ, ẓ, hard.

English.	Arabic.	Pronunciation.
beloved	عزيز	ʻazīz
better	احسن	aḥsan
bitter	مر	murr
blind	اعمى	aʻma
blunt (not sharp)	غير ماضي	ghair māḍi
blunt (in manner)	خشن الجانب	khashin-l-jānib
bold	جسور	jasūr
brave	شجاع	shujāʻ
bright, polished	لامع	lāmiʻ
broad	عريض	ʻarīḍ
busy	مشغول	mashghūl
careful	منتبه	muntabih
careless	غافل	ghāfil
certain, sure	اكيد	akīd
cheap	رخيص	rakhīṣ
clean	نظيف	naẓīf
clear	صافي	ṣāfi
clever	شاطر	shāṭir
cold	بارد	bārid
comfortable	مرتاح	murtāḥ
costly, dear	غالي	ghāli
damp	رطب	raṭib
dangerous	مخطر	mukhṭir
dark	معتم	muʻtim
deaf	اطرش	aṭrash
dear	حبيب	ḥabīb
deceitful	غشّاش	ghashshāsh

Vowel sounds: hat, fāther, bit, machīne, put, rūle, aisle; **au** = **ow** in cow
Dotted consonants, ḥ, ḍ, ṣ, ṭ, ẓ, **hard.**

ENGLISH.	ARABIC.	PRONUNCIATION.
deep	عميق ـ غويط	ʻamīq, ghawīṭ
delightful	بهيج ـ مفرّح	bahij, mufarriḥ
different	مختلف	mukhtalif
difficult	صعب	ṣaʻb
dirty	وسخ	wasikh
disagreeable	مكروه	makrūh
discreet	ذو تمييز	dhū tamyīz
dry	ناشف ـ يابس	nāshif, yābis
dull, stupid	بليد	balīd
dusty	مغبّر	mughabbar
early	مبكّر	mubakkir
easy	هيّن	haiyin
eldest	الكبير	al-kabīr
empty	فارغ	fārigh
every	كلّ واحد	kull wāḥid
faithful	امين	amīn
false	كاذب	kādhib
fashionable	حسب العادة	ḥasab-l-ʻādah
fat	سمين	samīn
few	قليل	qalīl
filthy	دنس	danis
fine (not coarse)	ناعم	nāʻim
fit	موافق	muwāfiq
flat	منبسط	munbasiṭ
foolish	جاهل	jāhil
fortunate	سعيد	saʻīd
free	حرّ	ḥurr

Vowel sounds: hat, fāther, bit, machīne, put, rūle, aisle; au = ow in cow.
Dotted consonants, ḥ, ḍ, ṣ, ṭ, ẓ, hard.

ENGLISH.	ARABIC.	PRONUNCIATION.
frequent	متكرر	mutakarrar
fresh	جديد	jadīd
friendly	مصادق	muṣādiq
full	ملان	mal'ān
gay	فرح	fariḥ
generous	كريم	karīm
glad	فرحان	farḥān
good	طيّب	ṭaiyib
great	عظيم - كبير	'azīm, kabīr
guilty	مجرم	mujrim
happy	سعيد	sa'īd
hard (cruel)	قاسى	qāsi
hard (dry)	يابس	yābis
healthy	متعافي	mut'āfi
heavy	ثقيل	thaqīl
high	عالي	'āli
honest	صادق	ṣādiq
hot	حارّ - سخن	ḥārr, sukhun
hungry	جوعان	ju'ān
ill (sick)	عيّان - مريض	'aiyān, marīḍ
impertinent	وقح	waqiḥ
important	مهمّ	muhimm
interesting	مفيد	mufīd
just	عادل	'ādil
kind	لطيف	laṭīf
large	كبير	kabīr
last	الاخير	al-akhīr

Vowel sounds: hat, fāther, bit, machīne, put, rūle, aisle; **au = ow** in cow
Dotted consonants, ḥ, ḍ, ṣ, ṭ, ẓ, **hard.**

ENGLISH.	ARABIC.	PRONUNCIATION.
late	متأخر	mut-akhkhir
lazy	كسلان	kaslān
lean	نحيف	naḥīf
least	الاقلّ	al-aqall
less	اقلّ	aqall
light (bright)	نيّر	naiyir
light (not heavy)	خفيف	khafīf
little (small)	صغير	ṣaghīr
long	طويل	ṭawīl
loose (not tight)	رخو	rakhu
loose (unbound)	محلول	maḥlūl
loud (shrill)	عالى	'āli
low	واطى	wāṭi
mad	مجنون	majnūn
many	كثيرين	kathīrīn
merry	فرحان	farḥān
narrow	ضيّق	ḍaiyiq
natural	طبيعى	ṭabi'i
new	جديد	jadīd
nice	ظريف	ẓarīf
old	قديم	qadīm
old man	شيخ	shaikh
open	مفتوح	maftūḥ
patient	صبور	ṣabūr
pleasant (man)	انيس	anīs
polite	اديب	adīb
poor	مسكين - فقير	maskīn, faqīr

Vowel sounds: hat, fāther, bit, machine, put, rūle, aisle; au = ow in cow.
Dotted consonants, ḥ, ḍ, ṣ, ṭ, ẓ, **hard.**

English.	Arabic.	Pronunciation.
possible	ممكن	mumkin
pretty	مليح	malīḥ
private	خصوصى	khuṣūṣi
probable	محتمل	muḥtamal
proud	متكبّر	mutakabbir
rash	عجول	'ajūl
ready	حاضر	ḥāḍir
rich	غنى	ghani
right and left	يميناً وشمالاً	yamīnan washimālan
right (correct)	صحيح	ṣaḥīḥ
ripe	مستوي	mustawi
round	مدوّر	mudauwar
rude	بلا ادب	bila adab
sacred	مقدّس	muqaddas
sad	حزين	ḥazīn
safe	آمن	āmin
shady	مظلّل	muẓallal
sharp (knife)	حادّ	ḥādd
short	قصير	qaṣīr
silent	ساكت	sākit
simple	بسيط	basīṭ
slow	بطىء	baṭī'
smooth	ملس	malis
soft	ناعم	nā'im
sore	موجع	mūji'
sound	سالم	sālim
sour	حامض	ḥāmiḍ

Vowel sounds: hat, fāther, bit, machīne, put, rūle, aisle; au = ow in cow.
Dotted consonants, ḥ, ḍ, ṣ, ṭ, ẓ, **hard.**

ENGLISH.	ARABIC.	PRONUNCIATION.
square	مربّع	murabba'
straight	مستقيم	mustaqīm
strange	غريب	gharīb
strong	قوي	qawi
sufficient	كافى	kāfi
sweet	حلو	ḥulu
tall	طويل	ṭawīl
thick	تخين	takhīn
thin	رقيق	raqīq
thirsty	عطشان	'aṭshān
tipsy	سكران	sakrān
tired	تعبان	ta'bān
true	حقّ	ḥaqq
ungrateful	كنود	kanūd
unintelligible	غير مفهوم	ghair mafhūm
unlucky	نحس	naḥs
useful	نافع	nāfi'
usual	اعتيادي	i'tiyādi
valuable	ثمين	thamīn
various	متنوّع	mŭtanauwi'
warm	سخن	sukhun
weak	ضعيف	ḍa'īf
well	طيّب	ṭaiyib
wet	مبلول	mablūl
wicked	شرّير	sharrīr
wide	واسع	wāsi'
wild	برّي	barri

Vowel sounds: hat, fāther, bit, machīne, put, rūle, aisle; au = ow in cow.
Dotted consonants, ḥ, ḍ, ṣ, ṭ, ẓ, **hard.**

English.	Arabic.	Pronunciation.
willing	راضى	rāḍi
wise	حكيم	ḥakīm
worse	اردا	arda
wrong	غلط	ghalaṭ
young	صغير	ṣaghīr

Verbs.[1]

abandon	ترك	tarak[2]
accept	قبل	qabil,[2] *imp.* iqbal
admire	تعجّب	ta'ajjab
agree to	اتّفق علي	ittafaq 'ala
allow	اذن - سمح	adhin, samaḥ
alter	غيّر	ghaiyar, *imp.* [ghaiyir
answer	جاوب	jāwab
appear	ظهر	ẓahar
arrive	وصل	waṣal
ask	سأل	sa'al, *imp.* is'al
assist	ساعد	sā'ad
avoid	اجتنب	ijtanab, *imp.* [ijtanib
awake	صحا	ṣaḥa
bathe (*trans.*)	حمّم	ḥammam
bathe (*intrans.*)	تحمّم	taḥammam
beat	ضرب	ḍarab, *imp.* iḍrib
become	صار	ṣār

[1] In grammars and dictionaries the 3rd masc. sing. past indic. is given as the root-form of the Arabic verb, and the same plan is followed here.

[2] Literally 'he abandoned', 'he accepted', and so forth.

ENGLISH.	ARABIC.	PRONUNCIATION.
begin	ابتداء	ibtada
believe	صدّق	ṣaddaq
bind (to tie)	ربط	rabaṭ, *imp.* urbuṭ
bite	عضّ	ʻaḍḍ
boil (*trans.*)	غلى	ghala
boil (*intrans.*)	انغلى	inghala
borrow	اقترض	iqtaraḍ
break	كسر	kasar
break to pieces	كسّر	kassar
bring	جاب	jāb, *imp.* jīb
build	بنى	bana
burn	حرق	ḥaraq
bury	دفن	dafan
buy	اشترى	ishtara
call	نادى	nāda
carry	حمل	ḥamal
catch	مسك	masak
change	غيّر	ghaiyar
change money	صرف	ṣaraf
cheat	غشّ	ghashsh
choose	اختار	ikhtār
clean	نظّف	naẓẓaf
climb	تسلّق	tasallaq
come	جاءَ	jā'a
come in	دخل	dakhal
consent	قبل	qabil
consult	شاور	shāwar

Vowel sounds: hat, fāther, bit, machīne, put, rūle, aisle; **au = ow** in cow
Dotted consonants, ḥ, ḍ, ṣ, ṭ, ẓ, **hard.**

ENGLISH.	ARABIC.	PRONUNCIATION.
convey	نقل	naqal
cook	طبخ	ṭabakh
cough	سعل	sa'al
count	عدّ - حسب	'add, ḥasab
cry	صرخ - بكى	ṣarakh, baka
cut	قطع	qaṭa'
dance	رقص	raqaṣ
deceive	خدع	khada'
decide	حتم	ḥatam
deliver	سلّم	sallam
deny	انكر	ankar
dislike	كره	karih
dismiss, drive out	طرد	ṭarad
dream	حلم	ḥalam
dress	لبس	labas
drink	شرب	sharib
eat	اكل	akal, *imp.* kul
examine	فحص	faḥaṣ
excavate	حفر	ḥafar
exceed	زاد	zād
exchange	بادل	bādal
excuse	عذر	'adhar
explain	وضّح	waḍḍaḥ
feed	اطعم	aṭ'am
feel	حسّ	ḥass
fetch	جاب	jāb, *imp.* jīb
find	وجد	wajad

Vowel sounds: hat, fāther, bit, machīne, put, rūle, aisle; au = ow in cow.
Dotted consonants, ḥ, ḍ, ṣ, ṭ, ẓ, hard.

ENGLISH.	ARABIC.	PRONUNCIATION.
forget	نسى	nasa
get in	دخل	dakhal
,, off	انطلق	inṭalaq
,, out	خرج	kharaj
,, up	قام	qām
give	اعطى	a'ṭa
go	راح	ḥrā
,, (on foot)	راح ماشى	rāḥ māshi
,, (on horseback)	راح راكب	rāḥ rakib
govern, rule	حكم	ḥakam
graze	رعى	ra'a
grease	دهن	dahan
hand	ناول	nawal
hang (*trans.*)	علّق	'allaq
hang(on gallows)(*trs.*	شنق	shanaq
happen	حصل	ḥaṣal
hear	سمع	sama'
help	ساعد	sā'ad
hide	خبّى	khabba
hire	اجّر	ajjar
hurry	استعجل	ista'jal
jump	نطّ	naṭṭ
kill	قتل	qatal
kiss	باس - قبّل	bās, qabbal
knock	دقّ	daqq
know	عرف	'araf
laugh	ضحك	ḍaḥik

Vowel sounds: **bat, fāther, bit, machīne, put, rūle, aisle; au=ow** in co
Dotted consonants, ḥ, ḍ, ṣ, ṭ, ẓ, **hard.**

English.	Arabic.	Pronunciation.
leap	نطّ	naṭṭ
learn	تعلّم	ta'allam
lend	اقرض	aqraḍ
let alone	خلّى	khalla
lie down	رقد - نام	raqad, nām
look	شاف - نظر	shāf, naẓar
make	عمل	'amil
meet	صادف	ṣādaf
mend	صلّح	ṣallaḥ
mention	ذكر	dhakar
mix	خلط	khalaṭ
move (*trans.*)	حرّك	ḥarrak
move (*intrans.*)	تحرّك	taḥarrak
obey	اطاع	aṭā'
object	اعترض	i'taraḍ
oblige (favour)	عمل معروف	'amil ma'rūf
obtain	نال	nāl
offend	اغضب	aghḍab
offer	قدّم	qaddam
omit	ترك	tarak
open (*trans.*)	فتح	fataḥ
open (*intrans.*)	انفتح	infataḥ
oppose	قاوم	qāwam
order	امر	amar
pack	حزم	ḥazam
pay	دفع	dafa'
perspire	عرق	'ariq

Vowel sounds: hat, fāther, bit, machīne, put, rūle, aisle; **au = ow** in cow. *Dotted consonants,* ḥ, ḍ, ṣ, ṭ, ẓ, **hard.**

English.	Arabic.	Pronunciation
play	لعب	la'ib
pour	صبّ	ṣabb
prepare	حضّر	ḥaḍḍar
prevent	منع	mana'
proceed	تقدّم	taqaddam
promise	وعد	wa'ad
pronounce	لفظ	lafaẓ
prosper	نجح	najaḥ
pull	جرّ	jarr
push	دفع	dafa'
put	حطّ	ḥaṭṭ
rains (it)	تمطر	tamṭur
raise	رفع	rafa'
read	قرا	qara
receive	استلم	istalam
reckon	حسب	ḥasib
recommend	وصّى على	waṣṣa 'ala
refuse	رفض	rafaḍ
reign	ملك	malak
rejoice	فرح	fariḥ
relate	حدّث	ḥaddath
remain	بقى	baqi
remember	تذكّر	tadhakkar
remind	ذكّر	dhakkar
repair	رمّم - صلّح	rammam, ṣal
repay	اوفى	aufa
repeat	كرّر	karrar

Vowel sounds: hat, fāther, bit, machīne, put, rūle, **aisle; au = ow** i
Dotted consonants, ḥ, ḍ, ṣ, ṭ, ẓ, **hard.**

ENGLISH.	ARABIC.	PRONUNCIATION.
reply	جاوب	jāwab
rest	استراح	istarāḥ
return (*trans.*)	ارجع	arja‘
return (*intrans.*)	رجع	raja‘
ride	ركب	rakib
ring (bell)	دقّ	daqq
rise	قام	qām
rub	فرك	farak
run	ركض	rakaḍ
run away	هرب	harab
save	خلّص	khallaṣ
say	قال	qāl
see	شاف	shāf
seize	مسك	masak
select	انتخب	intakhab
sell	باع	bā‘
send	ارسل	arsal
send back	رجّع	rajja‘
sew	خيّط	khaiyaṭ
share	شارك	shārak
shave	حلق	ḥalaq
shoot	قوّس	qauwas
shut	سدّ	sadd
sing	غنّى	ghanna
sit	قعد	qa‘ad
sleep	نام	nām
smell	شمّ	shamm

ENGLISH.	ARABIC.	PRONUNCIATION.
smoke	دخّن	dakhkhan
sneeze	عطس	ʻaṭas
speak	تكلّم	takallam
spend	صرف	ṣaraf
spoil (corrupt)	اتلف	atlaf
spoil (rob)	نهب	nahab
stand	وقف	waqaf
starve	مات من الجوع	māt min-l-jūʻ
stay	مكث	makath
steal	سرق	saraq
stop (*trans.*)	وقّف	waqqaf
stop (*intrans.*)	وقف	waqaf
study	درس	daras
suffer	تألّم	ta'allam
suggest	اشار	ashār
swallow	بلع	balaʻ
swear	حلف	ḥalaf
swim	سبح	sabaḥ
take	اخذ	akhadh
take care	اعتنى	iʻtana
taste	ذاق	dhāq
teach	علّم	ʻallam
tear	مزّق	mazzaq
tell	قال	qāl
thank	شكر	shakar
think	افتكر	iftakar
throw away	رمى	rama

Vowel sounds: hat, fāther, bit, machīne, put, rūle, aisle; **au=ow** in
Dotted consonants, ḥ, ḍ, ṣ, ṭ, ẓ, **hard.**

ENGLISH.	ARABIC.	PRONUNCIATION.
translate	ترجم	tarjam
travel	سافر	sāfar
tread	داس	dās
try	جرّب	jarrab
turn round	دار	dār
understand	فهم	fahim
use	استعمل	ista'mal
wait	صبر	ṣabar
walk	مشى	masha
want	احتاج	iḥtāj
warm	سخّن	sakhkhan
warn	نبّه	nabbah
wash	غسّل	ghassal
waste (lavish)	اسرف	asraf
watch	سهر	sahir
water	سقى	saqa
wear (put on)	لبس	labis
weigh	وزن	wazan
wet	بلّ	ball
whip	جلد	jalad
whisper	وشوش	washwash
whistle	صفّر	ṣaffar
win	ربح	rabiḥ
wipe	مسح	masaḥ
wish	اراد	arād
work	اشتغل	ishtaghal
worship	عبد	'abad

Vowel sounds: **hat, fāther, bit, machīne, put, rūle, aisle; au = ow in cow.**
Dotted consonants, ḥ, ḍ, ṣ, ṭ, ẓ, **hard.**

ENGLISH.	ARABIC.	PRONUNCIATION
wound	جرح	jaraḥ
wrap	لفّ	laff
write	كتب	katab
yawn	تثاوب	tathāwab
yield (produce)	انتج	antaj
yield (surrender)	خضع	khaḍa'

Vowel sounds: hat, fāther, bit, machīne, put, rūle, aisle; **au = ow** in co
Dotted consonants, ḥ, ḍ, ṣ, ṭ, ẓ, **hard.**

OUTLINE OF GRAMMAR.

Arabic grammar treats of—

Etymology, الصرف al-sarf, *the science of the formation of words, and* Syntax, النحو al-nahu, *the science of the formation of sentences.*

The Arabs have only three parts of speech—

I. الاسم al-ism, *the noun.*

II. الفعل al-fi'l, *the verb.*

III. الحرف al-harf, *the particle.*

The 'noun' includes the following seven forms :—

1. الاسم al-ism, *the noun* or *substantive.*
2. الضمير al-ḍamīr, *the personal pronoun.*
3. اسم الاشاره ism-l-ishārah, *the demonstrative pronoun.*
4. الاسم الموصول al-ism-l-mauṣūl, *the relative pronoun.*
5. اسم الاستفهام ism-l-istifhām, *the interrogative pronoun.*
6. اسم الصفه ism-l-ṣifah, *the adjective.*
7. اسم العدد ism-l-'adad, *the numeral adjective.*

I. THE NOUN.

The Arabs classify nouns as follows :—

(*a*) اسم جامد ism jāmid, *primitive noun.*

(*b*) اسم مشتق ism mushtaqq, *derived noun* (from verbs or nouns).

(*c*) اسم مجرد ism mujarrad, *noun of root-letters only.*

(*d*) اسم مزيد ism mazīd, *noun which is augmented by one or more letters, 'servile' or auxiliary.*[1]

(*e*) اسم علم ism 'alam, *proper noun,* to which the article ال al is never prefixed.

[1] See page 76.

(*f*) اسم جنس ism jins, *common noun*, which may be either—
اسم عَيّن ism ʻain, *noun denoting concrete object*, or
اسم معنى ism maʻna, *noun denoting an abstract idea.*

Primitive Noun.

A primitive noun, which is always a substantive, is one w has a pure root-form and is not derived from any verbal roo رجل rajul, *man*, موسى musa, *razor*, سفرجل safarjal, *quince.*

Derivative Noun.

A derivative noun is one which is constructed from a verb noun-root by the addition of one or more of the ten servile lett as اسلام Islām from سلم salima (*he is free from defect*), and ma either substantive or adjective. There are fourteen deriva nouns—

1. اسم المصدر ism-l-maṣdar, noun of action or infinitive, as ب ḍarb, *striking*, from ضَرَبَ ḍaraba, *he struck*; سُهُولة suhū *ease*, from سَهُلَ sahula, *to be at ease*; استغفار istighfār, *as forgiveness*, from استغفر istaghfara, *he asked forgiveness.*
2. اسم الفاعل ism-l-fāʻil, noun of agent or active participl ضارب ḍārib, *one who beats*, from ضَرَبَ ḍaraba, *he beat.*
3. اسم المفعول ism-l-mafʻūl, noun of object or passive partici as مضروب maḍrūb, *one who is beaten.*
4. اسم المكان والزمان ism-l-makān wal-zamān, noun of place time, as ملعب malʻab, *place* or *time of play*, from ب laʻiba, *he played.*
5. اسم آلة ism ālah, noun of instrument, as مِبْرَد mibrad, from بَرَدَ *he filed*; مِفْتاح miftāḥ, *key*, from فَتَحَ fataḥa *opened*; مكنسة miknasah, *broom*, from كنس kanasa, *he su*

---

[1] See page 76.

6. اسم المرّة ism-l-marrah, noun of unity, which expresses the doing of an action once. It is formed from triliteral verbs, as ضربة ḍarbah, *one blow*, from ضرب ḍaraba, *he struck.*

7. اسم النوع ism-l-nau', noun of kind and manner, as رِكبة rikbah, *manner of riding*, from ركب rakiba, *he rode.*

8. المصدر الميمي al-maṣdar-l-mīmī, noun of action with م m, as منطق manṭiq, *speaking*, from نطق naṭaqa, *he spoke.*

9. اسم التصغير ism-l-taṣghīr, diminutive noun, as كُلَيْب kulaib, *a little dog*, from كَلْب kalb, *a dog.*

10. الصفة المشبّهة باسم الفاعل al-ṣifat-l-mushabbahat bism-l-fā'il, adjective resembling noun of agent, as حَسَن ḥasan, *handsome*, from حَسُن ḥasuna, *he is handsome*; احمر aḥmar, *red*, from حَمُر, *he is red*; سيّد saiyid, *master*, from ساد sāda, *he ruled.*

1. اسم التفضيل ism-l-tafḍīl, noun of superiority for the comparative and superlative degrees, as احسن aḥsan, *more handsome*, الاحسن al-aḥsan, *most handsome*, both from حَسَن ḥasan, *handsome.*

2. اسم المبالغة ism-l-mubalaghah, noun of excess (to express intensity), as غفّار ghaffār, *one who pardons much*, from غافِر ghāfir, *pardoner.*

3. فعول وفعيل fa'ūl wa fa'īl. The two forms may be either noun of agent, as صَبُور ṣabūr, *patient*, مريض marīḍ, *sick*, or noun of object, as رَسُول rasūl, *apostle*, جريح jarīḥ, *wounded.*

4. الاسم المنسوب al-ism-l-mansūb, relative adjective, which is formed by affixing يّ to the noun, as رجل rajul, *man*, becomes رَجُلِي rajulī, *manly*; شمس shams, *sun*, becomes شَمْسِيّ shamsī, *solar*; انكليز inglīz, *English*, becomes انكليزيّ inglīzi, *English* (adjective).

Personal Pronouns.

Personal pronouns are either separate or suffixed. The *Sep*
Personal Pronouns, الضمائر المنفصلة, have the following form

Nominative Case.

	Sing.	Dual.	Plur.
1st pers.	أَنَا	نَحْنُ	نَحْنُ
2nd pers. masc. .	أَنْتَ	أَنْتُمَا	أَنْتُمْ
fem. . .	أَنْتِ	أَنْتُمَا	أَنْتُنَّ
3rd pers. masc. . .	هُوَ	هُمَا	هُمْ
fem. . .	هِيَ	هُمَا	هُنَّ

Accusative Case.

	Sing.	Dual.	Plur.
1st pers.	إِيَّايَ	إِيَّانَا	إِيَّانَا
2nd pers. masc. . .	إِيَّاكَ	إِيَّاكُمَا	إِيَّاكُمْ
fem. . .	إِيَّاكِ	إِيَّاكُمَا	إِيَّاكُنَّ
3rd pers. masc. . .	إِيَّاهُ	إِيَّاهُمَا	إِيَّاهُمْ
fem. . .	إِيَّاهَا	إِيَّاهُمَا	إِيَّاهُنَّ

The *Suffixed* or *Annexed Personal Pronouns*, مائر المتّصلة
when attached to a noun or preposition denote the genitive
but when attached to a verb they denote the accusative
They have the following forms:—

	Sing.	Dual.	Plur.
1st pers. to noun . .	ـِي	نَا	نا
to verb . .	نِي	نَا	نَا
2nd pers. masc. to both	كَ	كُمَا	كُمْ
fem. ,,	كِ	كُمَا	كُنَّ
3rd pers. masc. ,,	هُ	هُمَا	هُمْ
fem. ,,	هَا	هُمَا	هُنَّ

The *Annexed Personal Pronouns* which are attached to verbs only have the following forms and denote the nominative case :—

	SING.	DUAL.	PLUR.
1st pers.	تُ	نَا	نَا
2nd pers. masc. . .	تَ	تُمَا	تُمْ
fem. . .	تِ	تُمَا	تُنَّ
3rd pers.	none	ا	ـُوْا

Example of Personal Pronouns attached to the noun كتاب (book).

	SING.	DUAL.	PLUR.
1st pers.	كتابي	كتابنا	كتابنا
2nd pers. masc. . .	كتابكَ	كتابكما	كتابكم
fem. . .	كتابكِ	كتابكما	كتابكم
3rd pers. masc. . .	كتابهُ	كتابهما	كتابهم
fem. . .	كتابها	كتابهما	كتابهنّ

The English of the above is :

	SING.	DUAL.	PLUR.
1st pers.	*my book*	*our book* (when two are speaking)	*our book* (when three and more are speaking)

and so forth.

Example of Personal Pronouns attached to the verb ضرب (he struck), *denoting the Accusative Case.*

	SING.	DUAL.	PLUR.
1st pers.	ضربني	ضربنا	ضربنا
2nd pers. masc. . .	ضربكَ	ضربكما	ضربكم
fem. . .	ضربكِ	ضربكما	ضربكم
3rd pers. masc. . .	ضربهُ	ضربهما	ضربهم
fem. . .	ضربها	ضربهما	ضربهنّ

The English of the above is:

	SING.	DUAL.	PLUR.
1st pers.	*he struck me*	*he struck us*	*he struck us*

and so forth.

Example of Personal Pronouns annexed to the verb ضرب (he struc
denoting the Nominative Case.

	SING.	DUAL.	PLUR.
1st pers.	ضَرَبْتُ	ضَرَبْنَا	ضَرَبْنَا
2nd pers. masc. . .	ضَرَبْتَ	ضَرَبْتُمَا	ضَرَبْتُم
fem. . .	ضَرَبْتِ	ضَرَبْتُمَا	ضَرَبْتُنَّ
3rd pers. masc. . .	ضَرَبَ (pron. understood)	ضَرَبَا	ضَرَبُوا
fem. . .	ضَرَبَتْ (pron. understood; تْ is the sign of fem.)	ضَرَبَتَا	ضَرَبْنَ (نَ is the sign of fen

The English of the above is:

	SING.	DUAL.	PLUR.
1st pers.	*I have struck*	*we have struck*	*we have struck*

etc., etc.

Example of Personal Pronouns attached to the preposition مِنْ (fro

	SING.	DUAL.	PLUR.
1st pers.	مِنِّي	مِنَّا	مِنَّا
2nd pers. masc. . . .	مِنْكَ	مِنْكُمَا	مِنْكُم
fem. . . .	مِنْكِ	مِنْكُمَا	مِنْكُنَّ
3rd pers. masc. . . .	مِنْهُ	مِنْهُمَا	مِنْهُم
fem. . . .	مِنْهَا	مِنْهُمَا	مِنْهُنَّ

The English of the above is:

	SING.	DUAL.	PLUR.
1st pers.	*from me*	*from us*	*from us*

etc., etc.

Demonstrative Pronouns.

This (the near object).

		Masc.	Fem.
Sing.		ذَا	ذه, ذي, تِهِ, تَا, تِي
Dual	nom.	ذَانِ	تَانِ
	gen., acc.	ذَيْنِ	تَيْنِ
Plur.		أُولَاءِ or أُولَى	أُولَاءِ or أُولَى

This simple demonstrative pronoun may have the particle هَا, or oftener the defective هٰ, prefixed to it, as:

		Masc.	Fem.
Sing.		هٰذَا	هٰذِهِ, هٰذِي
Dual	nom.	هٰذَانِ	هٰتَانِ
	gen., acc.	هٰذَيْنِ	هٰتَيْنِ
Plur.		هٰؤُلَاءِ	هٰؤُلَاءِ

That (the middle and distant object).

	Masc.	Fem.
Sing.	ذٰلِكَ, ذَاكَ	تِلْكَ, تَاكَ, تِيكَ
Plur.	أُولَاكَ or أُولَائِكَ	أُولَاكَ or أُولَائِكَ

Relative Pronouns.

Who, which, that.

		Masc.	Fem.
Sing.		اَلَّذِي	اَلَّتِي
Dual	nom.	اَللَّذَانِ	اَللَّتَانِ
	gen., acc.	اَللَّذَيْنِ	اَللَّتَيْنِ
Plur.		اَلَّذِينَ	اَللَّوَاتِي or اَللَّاتِي

or اَللَّاءِ for both masc. and fem.

Other relative pronouns are : مَنْ *he* or *she who* ; مَا *that wh*
أَيٌّ (أَيَّةٌ fem.) *he who, she who, whoever* ; أَيُّمَنْ *he who, she*
whosoever ; أَيُّمَا *that which, whatsoever.*

Interrogative Pronouns.

مَنْ *who?* أَيٌّ (أَيَّةٌ fem.) *who?* مَا *what?* (and when jo
with the demonstrative ذَا becomes stronger, مَاذَا, *what ther*
كَمْ *how much?*

Numeral Adjectives.

1. The Cardinal Numbers.

The cardinal numbers from 1 to 10 have the following f
and are declinable. From 3 to 10 they take the fem. form w
the objects numbered are masc. gender, and conversely
masc. form when the objects numbered are fem.

		Masc.	Fem.			Masc.	F
1	(١)	وَاحِد	وَاحِدَة	5	(٥)	خَمْس	ـسَة
		أَحَد	إِحْدَى	6	(٦)	سِتّ	
2	(٢)	إِثْنَانِ	إِثْنَتَان	7	(٧)	سَبْع	ـة
			ثِنْتَان	8	(٨)	ثَمَان	ـيَة
3	(٣)	ثَلَاث	ثَلَاثَة	9	(٩)	تِسْع	ـة
4	(٤)	أَرْبَع	أَرْبَعَة	10	(١٠)	عَشْر	ـة

The numbers from 11 to 19 are indeclinable and have
following forms :—

		Masc.	Fem.
11	(١١)	أَحَدَ عَشَرَ	إِحْدَى عَشْرَةَ
12	(١٢)	إِثْنَا عَشَرَ	إِثْنَتَا عَشْرَةَ

	Masc.	Fem.
13 (١٣)	ثَلَاثَةَ عَشَرَ	ثَلَاثَ عَشْرَةَ
14 (١٤)	أَرْبَعَةَ عَشَرَ	أَرْبَعَ عَشْرَةَ
15 (١٥)	خَمْسَةَ عَشَرَ	خَمْسَ عَشْرَةَ
16 (١٦)	سِتَّةَ عَشَرَ	سِتَّ عَشْرَةَ
17 (١٧)	سَبْعَةَ عَشَرَ	سَبْعَ عَشْرَةَ
18 (١٨)	ثَمَانِيَةَ عَشَرَ	ثَمَانِي عَشْرَةَ
19 (١٩)	تِسْعَةَ عَشَرَ	تِسْعَ عَشْرَةَ

The numbers 20 - 90 are declinable. Their forms are: 20 عِشْرُونَ , 30 ثَلَاثُونَ , 40 أَرْبَعُونَ , 50 خَمْسُونَ , 60 سِتُّونَ, 70 سَبْعُونَ, 80 ثَمَانُونَ, 90 تِسْعُونَ, in the nominative case. In the accusative and genitive cases the ـون changes into ـين, as عِشْرِينَ. 100 مِائَة or مِئَة, 200 مِائَتَانِ, 300 ثَلَاثُ مِائَةٍ, 400 أَرْبَعُ مِائَةٍ, 500 خَمْسُ مِائَةٍ, 600 سِتُّ مِائَةٍ, 700 سَبْعُ مِائَةٍ, 800 ثَمَانِي مِائَةٍ, 900 تِسْعُ مِائَةٍ, 1,000 أَلْفٌ, 2,000 أَلْفَانِ, 3,000 ثَلَاثَةُ آلَافٍ, 100,000 مِائَةُ أَلْفٍ, 1,000,000 أَلْفُ أَلْفٍ.

2. The Ordinal Numbers.

The ordinal number 1 has the form فَعَّل, the numbers from 2 upwards have the form of the noun of the agent, فَاعِل, and are as follows:—

	Masc.	Fem.		Masc.	Fem.
1	أَوَّل	أُولَى	6	سَادِس	سَادِسَة
2	ثَانِي	ثَانِيَة	7	سَابِع	سَابِعَة
3	ثَالِث	ثَالِثَة	8	ثَامِن	ثَامِنَة
4	رَابِع	رَابِعَة	9	تَاسِع	تَاسِعَة
5	خَامِس	خَامِسَة	10	عَاشِر	عَاشِرَة

11 حَادِى عَشَرَ (masc.), حَادِيَةَ عَشْرَةَ (fem.), etc., etc.

21 حَادِي وَعِشْرُونَ or الحادي والعشرون .

For "*in the seventh year* A.D." you say في سنةِ سبعٍ للميلاد
في السنةِ السابعة للميلاد .

3. Distributive Numerals

have the following forms: أُحَادُ *one by one,* مَثْنَى or ثُنَاءُ *two by two,* مَثْلَثُ or ثُلَاثُ *three by three,* مَرْبَعُ or رُبَاعُ *four by four,* مَعْشَرُ or عُشَارُ *ten by ten.*

II. THE VERB.

Most of the Arabic verbs are triliteral verbs (ثلاثي), i.e. their root-forms have only three letters; but there are also a good many quadriliteral verbs (رباعي), whose root-forms have four letters.

Both have many derived forms, through the addition to the root-form of one, two, or three servile letters (which are ten in number and together form the word سالتمونيها *you have asked about them*). All increase in verbs and nouns is effected by means of these letters.

Arab grammarians have only three tenses, including the imperative, which they call a tense. These three tenses are—

1. ماضى māḍi, *past tense,* which European grammarians call perfect or preterite tense.
2. مضارع muḍāri', *present* or *future tense,* which European grammarians call imperfect or aorist tense.
3. أمر amr, *imperative tense.*

(*a*) Triliteral verbs (المجرد الثلاثي) have the following measures, giving the above three tenses:—

أُفْعُلْ	يَفْعُلُ	فَعَلَ	(1)
إِفْعِلْ	يَفْعِلُ	فَعَلَ	(2)
إِفْعَلْ	يَفْعَلُ	فَعَلَ	(3)
إِفْعَلْ	يَفْعَلُ	فَعِلَ	(4)
أُفْعُلْ	يَفْعُلُ	فَعُلَ	(5)
إِفْعِلْ	يَفْعِلُ	فَعِلَ	(6)

Note that the verb فَعَلَ *he has done* is commonly used as the model, because the 3rd pers. masc. sing., preterite, active, is the root-form of the verb, whence the first radical of the triliteral verb is called الفا (the *fā*), the second العين (the *'ain*), and the third اللام (the *lām*).

(*b*) The derived forms from the triliteral verb (المزيد الثلاثيّ) are ten in number. These forms, as well as those derived from the quadriliteral verbs, express various modifications of the idea conveyed by the root-form. The following are the derived forms of the triliteral verb, giving from right to left the past, present or future, imperative, noun of action, active participle, and passive participle of the verb قَتَلَ, *he has killed* :—

مُقَتَّلٌ	مُقَتِّلٌ	تَقْتِيلٌ	قَتِّلْ	يُقَتِّلُ	قَتَّلَ	(1)
مُقَاتَلٌ	مُقَاتِلٌ	قِتَالٌ	قَاتِلْ	يُقَاتِلُ	قَاتَلَ	(2)
مُقْتَلٌ	مُقْتِلٌ	إِقْتَالٌ	أَقْتِلْ	يُقْتِلُ	أَقْتَلَ	(3)
مُتَقَتَّلٌ	مُتَقَتِّلٌ	تَقَتُّلٌ	تَقَتَّلْ	يَتَقَتَّلُ	تَقَتَّلَ	(4)
مُتَقَاتَلٌ	مُتَقَاتِلٌ	تَقَاتُلٌ	تَقَاتَلْ	يَتَقَاتَلُ	تَقَاتَلَ	(5)
مُنْقَتَلٌ	مُنْقَتِلٌ	إِنْقِتَالٌ	إِنْقَتِلْ	يَنْقَتِلُ	إِنْقَتَلَ	(6)
مُقْتَتَلٌ	مُقْتَتِلٌ	إِقْتِتَالٌ	إِقْتَتِلْ	يَقْتَتِلُ	إِقْتَتَلَ	(7)
none	مُقْتَلٌّ	إِقْتِلَالٌ	إِقْتَلِلْ	يَقْتَلُّ	إِقْتَلَّ	(8)

(9) إِسْتَقْتَلَ يَسْتَقْتِلُ إِسْتَقْتِلْ إِسْتِقْتَالٌ مُسْتَقْتِلٌ مُسْتَقْتَلٌ

(10) إِقْتَالَّ يَقْتَالُّ إِقْتَالِلْ إِقْتِيلَالٌ مُقْتَالٌّ none

(*c*) The quadriliteral verb (المجرّد الرباعيّ) has only one form:

فَعْلَلَ يُفَعْلِلُ فَعْلِلْ فَعْلَلَةٌ مُفَعْلِلٌ مُفَعْلَلٌ

(*d*) The derived quadriliteral verbs (المزيد الرباعيّ) have three forms:

(1) تَفَعْلَلَ يَتَفَعْلَلُ تَفَعْلَلْ تَفَعْلُلٌ مُتَفَعْلِلٌ مُتَفَعْلَلٌ

(2) إِفْعَنْلَلَ يَفْعَنْلِلُ إِفْعَنْلِلْ إِفْعِنْلَالٌ مُفْعَنْلِلٌ مُفْعَنْلَلٌ

(3) إِفْعَلَلَّ يَفْعَلِلُّ إِفْعَلِلَّ إِفْعِلَّالٌ مُفْعَلِلٌّ مُفْعَلَلٌّ

III. THE PARTICLES.

1. Prepositions.

بِ *in, at, by.*

تَ *by* (in an oath), as تَاللّٰهِ.

لِ *to, for.*

وَ *by* (in an oath).

كَ *as, like.*

إلى *to.*

حتّى *till, up to.*

عَلَى *over, above,* etc.

عن *from, after, for.*

في *in, into.*

لَدُنْ *with.*

مع *with.*

مِنْ *of, from.*

مُنْذُ or مُذْ *since.*

بَيْنَ *between.*

أمَامَ *before.*

بَعْدَ *after.*

تَحْتَ *under.*

حَوْلَ *round about.*

خَلْفَ *behind.*

عِنْدَ *with.*

عِوَضَ *for.*

فَوْقَ *above.*

قَبْلَ *before* (time).

قدّامَ *before* (place).

2. Adverbs.

أَ particle of interrogation.

سَ and سَوْفَ to express the future of the verb in the aorist tense.

لَ *certainly.*

إِذْ and إِذَا *lo!*

إِذَنْ *well then.*

إِنْ *verily.*

إِنَّ *certainly.*

أَيْ *that is.*

أَيْنَ *where?*

بَلْ *nay, but.*

بَلَى *yes.*

ثَمَّ *there.*

فَقَطْ *only.*

قَدْ *before* (past tense), *now.*

قَطُّ *ever.*

كَذَا or كَذٰلِكَ *likewise.*

كَلَّا *not at all.*

لٰكِنْ *but.*

مَتَى *when?*

نَعَمْ *yes.*

Etc., etc.

3. Conjunctions.

وَ and فَ *and.*

أَمْ and أَوْ *or.*

أَنْ *that.*

إِنْ *if.*

ثُمَّ *then.*

كَيْ and لِكَيْ *in order that.*

لَوْ *if.*

مَا *as long as.*

4. Interjections.

أَيُّهَا *O!*

هَلُمَّ *come here!*

هَيْهَاتَ *far from it!*

هَيَّا *make haste!*

بَخْ *well done!*

أُفٍّ *fie!*

صَهْ *hush!*

يَا *O!* (in *O God!* etc.).

وَيْحَ *woe to!*

هَاتِ *bring here!*

SYNTAX (النحو).

The signs of the declensions for the four cases are either vo or letters.

I. The *Nominative Case* has four signs—

1. ـُ (*a*) in the singular of the noun, as جاءَ الرَّجُلُ *the man* c

(*b*) in the irregular plural, as جاءَ الرِّجالُ *the men came.*

(*c*) in the regular feminine plural, as جاءَت المومنات *believers* (fem.) *came.*

(*d*) in the present-future tense of the verb, when not is annexed to its last letter, as يضربُ الرجلُ *the strikes* or *will strike* (this being really the indic mood).

2. و (*a*) in the regular masculine plural, as جاءَ المومنون *believers came.*

(*b*) in the following five nouns: أَب *father,* أَخ *bro* حَمُو *father-in-law,* فُوه *mouth,* ذُو *owner*; as ابوكَ واخوكَ وحموكَ وذو مالٍ ونطق فوكَ *thy father and thy brother and thy father-in-law and the own wealth, and thy mouth spoke.*

3. ا in the dual nouns, as جاءَ المومنان *the two believers cam*

4. ن in the present-future tense of the verb, when the pers pronoun of either the dual, or the plural, or singular of the second person feminine is annexe the verb; as الرجلانِ يضربانِ *the two men strik*

will strike, المراءتان تضربانِ *the two women strike* or *will strike,* الرجالُ يضربونَ *the men strike* or *will strike,* انتم تضربون *you strike* or *will strike,* انتِ تضربينَ *thou* (fem.) *strikest* or *wilt strike.*

II. The *Accusative Case* has five signs—

1. ـَ (*a*) in the singular noun, as ضربتُ الرجلَ *I struck the man.*
   (*b*) in the irregular plural, as ضربتُ الرجالَ *I struck the men.*
   (*c*) in the present-future tense of the verb, when nothing is annexed to its last letter, and when it is influenced by a word which governs the accusative, as لن يضربَ *he will never strike.*

2. ـِ in the regular feminine plural, as جاءَت النساءُ راكباتٍ *the women came riding.*

3. ا in the five nouns (اب, اخ, etc.), as رايتُ اخاكَ *I saw thy brother.*

4. ي in the regular masculine dual and plural nouns, as رايتُ الرجلَيْنِ *I saw the two men,* رايتُ المومنِيْنَ *I saw the believers.*

5. Suppression of the ن of the declension in the five verbs يضربانِ, تضربانِ, يضربونَ, تضربونَ, and تضربينَ, which become يضربا, تضربا, يضربوا, تضربوا, and تضربى ; as لن يرجعا *they two will never return.* Observe a superfluous alif is added to the third and fourth, called the guarding alif (الف الوقايه) or the separating alif (الالف الفاصله), which, however, disappears when a pronoun is annexed, and is never pronounced.

III. The *Genitive Case* has three signs—

1. ـِ (*a*) in the declinable singular noun, as ت في الكتابِ *I read in the book.*

(*b*) in the declinable irregular plural noun, as تُ للرجالِ *I said to the men.*

(*c*) in the regular plural feminine noun, as تُ للمومناتِ *I said to the believers* (fem.).

2. ـَ in the imperfectly declined noun, as قلتُ لاحمدَ *I said Ahmad.*

3. ي (*a*) in the five nouns (اب, اخ, etc.), as رت بابِيكَ *I passed thy father.*

(*b*) in the dual noun, as مررتُ بالكافرَيْنِ *I passed the unbelievers.*

(*c*) in the plural regular noun, as مررتُ بالمومنِينَ *I pas the believers.*

IV. The *Apocopative or Jussive Case*[1] (جزم) has three sign

1. ـْ in the present-future tense of the verbs ending with str letters (when not joined to expressed pronouns in nominative case), as لم اضربْ *I did not strike.*

2. Suppression of ن in the five verbs (see above, II, 5), as ـربَا *do not (ye two) strike.*

3. Suppression of weak letters, when verbs end in such and not joined to an expressed pronoun in the nominat case, as أَلَمْ تمشِ *did you not walk?*

[1] Conditional and imperative moods, or verbs following the apocopative parti

1. The Nominative Case (الرفع).

The following are in this case :—

1. The subject of the sentence (أَلْمُبْتَدَأ), as النومُ لذيذٌ *sleep is pleasant.*

2. The predicate of the sentence (أَلْخَبَر), as زيدٌ قَائِمٌ *Zaid is standing.*

3. The agent of the sentence (أَلْفَاعِل), as جَاءَ زَيْدٌ *Zaid came.*

4. The substitute for the agent (نائِبُ الفَاعِل), subject of a passive verb, as ضُرِبَ زَيْدٌ *Zaid was beaten.*

5. The subject of كَانَ and its sisters, as كان النهارُ مُظْلِمًا *the day was dark.*

6. The predicate of إِنَّ and its sisters, and of لَا (the absolute negative); as إِنَّ زيدًا راكبٌ *verily Zaid is riding,* لا إِنْسَانَ قَادِمٌ *there is no man coming.*

7. The present-future tense when not governed by particles nor followed by a fem. ن or an emphatic ن; as يكتبُ التلميذُ الدرسَ *the pupil writes the lesson.*

8. Nouns or adjectives in apposition to nominatives (توابع المرفوعات), as جاءَ الرجلُ الكريمُ *the generous man came.*

2. The Accusative Case (النصب).

The following are in the accusative case :—

1. Noun of action as absolute object (المفعول المطلق), as ضَرَبَ ضَرْبًا *he struck a striking,* i.e. *he assuredly struck.*

2. Noun of object of the transitive verb (المفعول بِهِ), as رَكِبَ الفَرَسَ *he rode the horse,* ضَرَبَنِي *he struck me* (the annexed personal pronoun being the objective complement).

3. Adverbial noun of time and place (المفعولُ فيهِ), with meaning as if it were preceded by the preposition فِي *in* جاءَ صباحًا *he came in the morning,* جاءَ امامَ القاضي *he came be the judge,* or *into his presence.*

4. Adjectival noun of state or condition (الحال), which m always be indefinite and derived, standing at the end of sentence, as جاءَ الاميرُ راكِبًا *the prince came riding.*

5. Noun of specification (التمييز) is always a common n explaining something that is uncertain as regards the substanc relation of a thing, as إشترى رطلاً خُبزًا *he bought a pound of br* كَرُمَ زيدٌ ابًا *Zaid is honourable as regards his father.*

6. Vocative noun (المنادَى) when it is a proper nc singular, then it is put in the nominative case, as يا زيدُ *O Za* but when it is not it takes the accusative, as يا رجلاً *O man!*

7. Noun of action of cause or reason (المفعولُ لهُ), as ب خوفًا *he fled from fright.*

8. Noun of object following وَ having the meaning of (المفعولُ مَعَهُ), as جاءَ الاميرُ وَالجَيْشَ *the prince came with the ar*

9. The noun which is excepted (المُستَثنَى) by means of غَيْرَ , سِوَى , عَدَا , خَلَا , حَاشَا ; as قَامَ القَوْمُ إِلَّا زَيْدًا *the people s except Zaid.*

10. The predicate of كان and of its sisters, as زيدٌ قائِمًا *Zaid was standing.*

11. The subject of إِنَّ and of its sisters, as زيدًا راكبٌ *verily Zaid is riding.*

12. The subject of لا the absolute negative, as لا إنسانَ قائِمٌ

13. Nouns or adjectives in apposition to accusatives (تابع المنصوبات), as رأيتُ زيدًا العاقلَ, *I saw Zaid the wise.*

3. The Genitive Case (الجَرّ).

1. Genitive by prepositions: whenever a noun is preceded by any of the following prepositions it is put in the genitive case: مِنْ ,إِلَى ,عَنْ ,عَلَى ,فِي ,رُبَّ ,بِ ,كَ ,لِ ,وَ ,تَ ,مُنْذُ ,مُذْ ,عِنْدَ, حَتَّى ,كَي ,خَلَا ,عَدَا ,حَاشَا ; as خَرَجَ مِنَ الدَّارِ *he went out from the house.*

2. When two nouns are in construction (or annexation), i.e. follow each other, and the second depends on the first, the second is put in the genitive case, i.e. takes kasra (ـِـ); as كِتَابُ رَجُلٍ *the book of a man,* كِتَابُ الرَجُلِ *the book of the man.* Note that in such a construction or annexation the first noun never takes the article أَلْ although it is understood.

3. Nouns in apposition to genitives take the genitive case, كِتَابُ الرَجُلِ العَظِيمِ *the book of the great man.*

The Verb in Syntax.

1. The past tense (preterite) is indeclinable and has always fatḥa (ـَـ) over the last letter, as ضَرَبَ *he struck.*

2. The imperative tense is also indeclinable and has always jasm (ـْـ) over the last letter, as اُقْتُلْ *kill.*

3. The present-future tense (aorist) has always one of the four servile letters ا, ن, ي, ت prefixed to it. It is limited to the present when preceded by the emphatic لَ, the negative مَا, or the verb لَيْسَ, and to the future when preceded by سَ for the near future, or سَوْفَ for the remote future.

It is always in raf' (ـُـ) nominative case, or, as we should say, indicative mood; as يَكْتُبُ *he writes,* or *he will write,* except when influenced by (*a*) one of the ten accusative particles preceding which are: أَنْ, لَنْ, إِذًا, كَيْ, the ل of كَيْ, the negative حَتّى, and the فَ, وَ, أَوْ, when preceding the apodosis (جواب when the tense takes the accusative case, or, as we should s when it is in the subjunctive mood; or (*b*) when the aorist influenced by jasm (ـْ) preceded by one of the apocopat particles, which are: لَمْ, لَمَّا, أَلَمْ, أَلَمَّا, the ل of command a entreaty, the لا of forbidding and entreaty, إِنْ, مَا, مَنْ, مَهْمَا, إِذْمَا, أَيّ, مَتَى, أَيَّانَ, أَيْنَ, أَنَّى, حَيْثُمَا, كَيْفَمَا, and إِذَا poetry. [In a conditional sentence of two clauses, the verb the first is called فعل الشرط, the protasis, and that of the sec جواب الشرط, the apodosis.]

To the Student.

In order to turn the following exercises to the great advantage, it is recommended that the student should learn th by heart, repeating each sentence aloud, with the aid of phonetic transcription in the third column, until it can be spo readily and easily, and the ear has grown accustomed to the sou Copying the sentences out will greatly facilitate learning. E section should in this way be mastered in turn, and this app equally to the conversational sentences on pp. 97–124.

After learning a section or group of sentences, the Eng words should be written down and the Arabic equivalents ad from memory. The result can then be checked by reference the book.

By following the above method, a great amount of use practice will be obtained in speaking, reading, and writing Ara whilst at the same time much conversational matter of a pract and valuable character will be acquired.

EXERCISES ON THE GRAMMAR.

1. The Preterite Tense.

ENGLISH.	ARABIC.	PRONUNCIATION.
I have received a letter	وصلنى مكتوب	waṣalni maktūb
He lost his watch	اضاع ساعته	aḍa'a sā'atuh
His friend gave it to him	اعطاهُ اياها صاحبه	a'ṭāhu īyāha ṣāḥibuh
You were not diligent	ما كنت مجتهدًا	ma kunta mujtahidan
You have been drinking again	عدتَ الى الشرب	'udta ila-l-shurb
I was about to begin my journey	هممت بان ابدا بسفرتي	hamamtu bian abda bisafrati
He did not bring the horse	لم يحضر الحصان	lam yuḥḍir-il-ḥiṣān
He has not long left us	ما غاب عنّا مدّة طويله	ma ghāb 'anna muddah awīlah
I was very late	انا كنت متأخرًا جدًا	ana kuntu mut'akhiran jiddan
You did not know of his arrival	ما كان لك علم بوصوله	ma kān lak 'ilm biwuṣūlihi
How long was he absent?	كم لبث غائبًا	kam labath aghāyiban?
He promised to come in an hour	وعد ان يحضر بعد ساعة	wa'ada an yaḥḍar ba'd sā'ah
Has he forgotten his promise?	أنسي وعدهُ	a-nasiya wa'dahu?
She was always punctual	هي كانت تراعي الميعاد دائمًا	hiya kanat turā'i-l-mī'ād dāyiman

Vowel sounds. hat, fāther, bit, machīne, put, rūle, aisle; au = ow in cow.
Dotted consonants, ḥ, ḍ, ṣ, ṭ, ẓ, hard.

English.	Arabic.	Pronunciation.
We lived in a house, not in a tent	سكنّا بيتًا لا خيمةً	sakanna baitan la khaimatan
They have always resided near the city	كل اقامتهم بالقرب من المدينه	kull iqāmathum bil-qurb mini-l-madīna
You have been stealing again	عدتَ الى السرقه	'udta ilas-sirqah
I went to (the) church this morning	ذهبت الى الكنيسه هذا الصباح	dhahabtu ila-l-kanīsah hādha-ṣ-ṣabāh
Who was there?	مَن كان هناك	man kan hunāk?
The bishop preached an eloquent sermon	وعظ المطران وعظه فصيحه	wa'aẓ-al-muṭrān wa'ẓah faṣīḥah
The collection amounted to ten pounds	بلغت اللمّه عشرة ليرات	balaghat-il-lammah 'asharat līrāt
With the sum they bought a bell for the church	اشتروا بالمبلغ جرسًا للكنيسه	ishtaru bil-mablagh jarasan lil-kanīsah
The doctor was not at home	لم يكن الطبيب في البيت	lam yakun il-ḍabīb fil-bait
His wife was in the [garden	كانت زوجته في البستان	kanat zaujatu fil-[bistān
Did you tell her to send the doctor as soon as he returns?	أقلت لها ان ترسل الطبيب حالما يرجع	a-kult laha an tursil-il-ṭabīb ḥālama yarja'?
Yes, and she gave me this medicine	نعم واعطتنى هذا الدوا	na'am waa'ṭatni hādha-l-dawa
You have done well	فعلت حسنًا	fa'alta ḥasanan
What have you done to-day?	ماذا عملت اليوم	mādha 'amilt-al-yaum?

Vowel sounds. hat, fāther, bit, machīne, put, rūle, aisle; au = ow in cow.
Dotted consonants, ḥ, ḍ, ṣ, ṭ, ẓ, hard.

English.	Arabic.	Pronunciation.
I sold all my goods	بعت بضاعتي كلّها	biʻt biḍāʻati kulla
Has he paid you for it ?	هل دفع لك حقّها	hal dafaʻlak ḥaqqa
I have heard a strange story to-day from the muleteer	انا سمعت اليوم قصّه غريبه من المكاري	ana samiʻtu-l-ya quṣṣah gharībah min-il-mukāri

2. The Aorist Tense.

I like riding	انا احبّ الركوب	ana uhibb-ul-rukū
You prefer walking	انت تفضّل المشي	anta tufaḍḍil-ul-ma
He eats very little in the evening	هو ياكل قليل جدًا في المساء	huwa yākul qalīl jiddan fil-masa
She sleeps long	هي تنام مدّه طويله	hiya tanām mud ṭawīlah [naum
He walks in his sleep	هو يمشي في نومه	huwa yamshi fi
We like our breakfast in the open	نحن نحبّ الفطور في الخلا	nahnu nuhibb-ul-fuṭūr fil-khala
You will never follow my advice	انت لا تتّبع نصيحتي ابدًا	anta la tattabiʻ na ḥati abadan
I never ride donkeys	انا لا اركب الحمير اصلاً	ana la arkabu-l-ḥan aṣlan [kadh
She hates lies	هي تبغض الكذب	hiya tabghuḍu-l-
They will have rainy weather to-day	سيكون لهم اليوم مطر	sayakūn lahum al-yaum maṭar
He cooks well	هو يطبخ جيّدًا	huwa yaṭbukh jaiyi
I want a glass of water	اريد كاس ماء	urīd kās mā
Do you wish to drink a glass of wine ?	أتريد تشرب قدح نبيذ	a-turīd tashrab qad nabīdh ?

Vowel sounds: **hat, fāther, bit, machīne, put, rūle, aisle; au = ow in cow**
Dotted consonants, **ḥ, ḍ, ṣ, ṭ, ẓ, hard.**

English.	Arabic.	Pronunciation.
She prefers a cup of coffee [now	هى تفضّل فنجان قهوه	hiya tufaḍḍil finjā qahwah [alā
They will not dine just	لا يريدوا يتغدّوا الآن	la yarīdu yatghadd
I shall not employ him any more	لا استخدمه فيما بعد ابدًا	la astakhdimhu fīm ba'd abadan
Will you not help me to pitch the tent?	هلّا تساعدني في نصب الخيمه	halla tusa'idni fī naṣb-il-khaimah?
He will go to the market next week	هو يذهب الى السوق الجمعه القادمه	huwa yadhhab ila-l sūq al-jum'a-l-qādim
We respect others	نحن نكرم الغير	naḥu nukrim-ul-ghai
Why will you not come with me? [you	لماذا لا تريد ان تجى معى	limādha lā turīd a taji ma'i?
They are laughing at	هم يضحكوا عليك	hum yaḍḥaku 'ala i
I will follow you	انا اتبعك	ana atba'ak
She will remain behind	هى تتخلّف	hiya tatkhallaf
When the clock strikes seven waken me	حين تدق الساعه سبعًا صحّينى	ḥīn taduq-ul-sa'ah sab'an ṣaḥḥīni
She has not finished her dinner yet	ما فرغت من غدائها بعد	ma faraghat min ghadā'iha ba'd
It is time to go to bed (time of sleep)	صار وقت النوم	ṣār waqt-ul-naum
You are strong	انت قوي	anta qawi
She is ill	هي مريضه	hiya marīḍah
England is a great country	بلاد الانكليز مملكه عظيمه	bilād-ul-inglīz mam lakah 'aẓīmah
The Arabs like the English	اولاد العرب يحبّون الانكليز	aulād-ul-'arab yaḥubbun-al- ingl

Vowel sounds: hat, fāther, bit, machīne, put, rūle, aisle; au = ow in cow.
Dotted consonants, ḥ, ḍ, ṣ, ṭ, ẓ, hard.

English.	Arabic.	Pronunciation.
The camel is the favourite animal in Arabia	الجمل هو الحيوان المحبوب في عربستان	al-jamal huwa-l-ḥaiwān-ul-maḥbūb fī 'arabistān
The road to Jericho is dangerous	الطريق الى اريحا مخطره	al-ṭarīq ila arīḥa mukhṭirah
You are right	الحق معك	al-ḥaqq ma'ak
He is in the wrong	الحق عليه	al-ḥaqq 'alaih

3. The Imperative Mood.

Do not sit	لا تقعد	lā taq'ud
Go quickly	اذهب حالاً	idhhab ḥālan
Do not forget what I told you	لا تنسَ ما قلتهُ لك	lā tansa mā qultuhu lak
Return here in half an hour	ارجع هنا بعد نصف ساعه	irja' huna ba'd niṣf sā'ah
Do not make me angry	لا تغضبني	lā tughḍibni
Let us go to the Mount of Olives	لنذهب الى جبل الزيتون	linadhhab ila jabal-il-zaitūn
Carry this bag on your back	احمل هذا الكيس على ظهرك	iḥmil hādha-l-kīs 'ala ẓahrak
Take these letters to the post	خذ هذه المكاتيب الى البوسطه	khudh hādhi-l-makātīb ila-l-bōsṭa
Do you know the name of this village?	ياترى تعرف اسم هذه القريه	yatara ta'rif ism hādhi-l-qiryah?
Clean my saddle	نظّف سرجي	naẓẓif sarji
Bring my rifle	جيب بارودتي	jīb bārūdati

Vowel sounds: **hat, fāther, bit, machīne, put, rūle, aisle; au = ow** in cow.
Dotted consonants, ḥ, ḍ, ṣ, ṭ, ẓ, **hard.**

English.	Arabic.	Pronunciation.
Put the luggage in my room	حطّ العفش في اوضتي	ḥuṭṭ-il-'afsh fi auḍati
Tell the maid to come to the drawing-room	قل للخادمه تحضر الى الديوان	qull lilkhādimah taḥḍar ila-l-dīwān
Dust the table and the windows	نظفي السفره والشبابيك من الغبار	naẓẓifi-l-sufrah wal-shabābīk min-il-ghibār
Prepare a dinner for six persons	حضّري غدا لستّة اشخاص	ḥaḍḍiri ghada lisittat ashkhāṣ
Let us sit down and make out the account of our expenditure	لنجلس ونعمل حساب مصروفنا .	linajlis wa-na'mal ḥisāb maṣrūfina
Cash this cheque	جيب قيمة هذه الحواله	jīb qīmat hādhi-l ḥiwālah
Be quick, before the bank closes	اسرع قبل ان يقفل البنك	isri' qabl an yaqfil il-bank

4. How the English Potential and Subjunctive Mood are expressed in Arabic.

I can read and write	انا اقدر اقرا واكتب	ana aqdar aqra wa aktub
She can ride, but you cannot	هي تقدر تركب وامّا أنت فلا	hiya taqdar tarkab wa-amma anta falā
John can lift this box on his shoulder	حنّا يقدر يرفع هذا الصندوق على كتفهِ	Hanna yaqdar yarfa' hādha-l-ṣandūq 'al kitfihi

Vowel sounds · hat, fāther, bit, machīne, put, rūle, aisle; au = ow in cow.
Dotted consonants, ḥ, ḍ, ṣ, ṭ, ẓ, hard.

English.	Arabic.	Pronunciation.
We cannot go out to-day on account of the heavy rain	لا نقدر نخرج اليوم بسبب المطر القوي	la naqdar nakhruj al-yaum bisabab-il-maṭar-il-qawi
Can you drink sour milk ?	ياترى تقدر تشرب لبن	yatara taqdar tashrab laban ?
You may like it	ربما تحبه	rubbama tuḥibbuh
He may go with me to the Mosque of Omar	يمكنه يرافقني الى الحرم الشريف	yumkinhu yurāfiqni ila-l-ḥaram-ish-sharīf
It may rain	ربما تمطر	rubbama tamṭur
She can wait	هي تستطيع ان تصبر	hiya tastaṭīʻ an taṣbur
Could I have come when I told him I would not ?	أقدرت ان اجى لما قلت له انى لا اجى	a-qadartu an ajī lamma qult lahu inni lā ajī ?
They might reject my advice	ربما يرفضوا نصيحتي	rubbama yarfuḍu naṣīḥati
You should learn Arabic	عليك ان تتعلم العربيه	ʻalaik an tatʻallam al-ʻarabīyah
It might help you	ربما تنفعك	rubbama tanfaʻak
Why should you neglect this opportunity ?	كيف تهمل هذه الفرصه	kaif tuhmil hādhi-l-furṣah ?
Can he have told you the truth ?	هل من الممكن انه قال لك الحق	hal min-il-mumkin innahu qāl laka-l-haqq ?
She cannot have seen him	غير ممكن انها رأته	ghair mumkin innaha raʼathu
He might have eaten a little more	كان يمكن له ان ياكل اكثر قليلا	kān yumkin lahu an yaʼkul akthar qalīlan

Vowel sounds. hat, fāther, bit, machīne, put, rūle, aisle; au = ow in cow.
Dotted consonants, ḥ, ḍ, ṣ, ṭ, ẓ, hard.

ENGLISH.	ARABIC.	PRONUNCIATION.
If I strike him he will complain of me to the Consul	ان اضربه يشكونى الى القنصل	in aḍribhu yashkūni ila-l-Cunsul
Unless you work better I will dismiss you from my service	ان لم تشتغل احسن فارفضك من خدمتى	in lam tashtagil aḥsan fa-arfuḍak min khidmati

5. The Participles.

Neglecting to take exercise, he became ill	باهماله للرياضه صار مريضاً	bi-ihmālihilil-riyāḍah ṣāra marīḍan
Having received two pounds, he bought a new suit of clothes	بعد ان اخد ليرتين اشترى بدله جديده	ba‘d an akhadh līra-tain ishtara badlah jadīdah
Grasping my hand, he shook it violently	بقبضهِ على يدي هزّها بشدّه	biqabḍihi ‘ala yadi hazzaha bishiddah

6. The position of Adverbs.

Have you ever seen Jerusalem?	هل زرتم القدس قط	hal zurtum-ul-kuds qaṭṭ?
Has she never eaten pomegranates before?	ألم تاكل رمّانًا اصلًا	a-lam tākul rum-mānan aṣlan?
This horse not only kicks, but also shies	هذا الحصان لا يرفس فقط بل يجفل ايضاً	hādha-l-ḥiṣān la yarfus faqaṭṭ bal yajfal aiḍan
He rides remarkably well	هو يركب احسن ما يكون	huwa yarkab aḥsan mā yakūn [qatan
She is truly grateful	هى شكوره حقيقةً	hiya shakūrah ḥaqī-

English.	Arabic.	Pronunciation.
Do I read plainly?	هل اقرا ببيان	hal aqra bibayān?
She dresses beautifully	هي تجيد في اللبس	hiya tujīd fil-libs
He writes fast	هو يكتب بسرعه	huwa yaktub bisur'ah
They see me daily	ينظروني كلّ يوم	yanẓurūni kull yaum
He studies diligently	يدرس باجتهاد	yadrus bi-ijtihād

7. The Infinitive Mood.

I intended to see you	نويت ان ازورك	nawait an azūrak
He was happy to see me	فرح لرؤيتى	fari a li-ru'yati
She ordered her to cook the rice well	امرتها بطبخ الرزّ جيّدًا	āmaratha biṭabkh-il-ruzz jaiyidan
It is right to speak the truth	التكلّم بالحقّ صواب	al-takallum bil-haqq ṣawāb
I was hoping to receive a present from you at Christmas	كنت ارجو ان انال هبة منك في عيد الميلاد	kuntu arju an anāl hibah minka fī 'īd-il-mīlād
He intended to buy my horse yesterday	ازمع مشترى فرسى امساً	azma'a mushtara farasi amsan
We were expecting you to fulfil your promise	كنّا ننتظر انجاز وعدكم	kunna nantaẓir injāz wa'dakum
To live in a hot country in the summer is not pleasant	المعيشه فى بلاد حارّه في الصيف غير مستطابه	al-ma'īshah fī bilād ḥārrah fil-ṣaif ghair mustaṭābah
One longs to see rain	الانسان يشتاق لرؤية المطر	al-insān yashtāq liru'yat-il-maṭar

Vowel sounds: **hat, fāther, bit, machīne, put, rūle, aisle; au = ow in cow.**
Dotted consonants, ḥ, ḍ, ṣ, ṭ, ẓ, **hard.**

English.	Arabic.	Pronunciation.
To drink beer in the heat is injurious to health	شرب البيرا فى الحرّ مضرّ بالصحّة	shurbu-l-bīra fil-ḥarr muḍirr bil-siḥḥah
He ought to have paid me my dues	كان ينبغى له ان يوفيني حقّى	kān yanbaghi lahu an yūfīni ḥaqqi
She is supposed to know how to cut out	يُظن فيها انّها تعرف التفصيل	yuẓan fīha annaha ta'raf-il-tafṣīl
He claims to have learned English in six months	يدعي انّه تعلّم الانكليزية في ستة شهور	yadda'i annahu ta'allam al-inglīzi-yah fī sittat shuhūr
To frighten strangers is very wrong	تخويف الغرباء خطاء عظيم	takhwīf-ul-ghuraba khaṭā 'aẓīm
To steal is sin	السرقة حرام	al-sirqah ḥarām
To love one's neighbour is God's command	محبّة الجار وصيّة الله	maḥabbat-ul-jār waṣiyat-ul-lāhi

Vowel sounds: hat, fāther, bit, machīne, put, rūle, aisle; **au = ow** in cow.
Dotted consonants, ḥ, ḍ, ṣ, ṭ, ẓ, **hard.**

CONVERSATIONAL PHRASES AND SENTENCES.*

Useful and Necessary Expressions.

ENGLISH.	ARABIC.	PRONUNCIATION.
Allow me	اسمح لى	ismaḥ li
Are you hungry?	انت جوعان	anta jau'ān ?
At last!	اخيرًا	akhīran !
Be careful	اعطى بالك	a'ṭi bālak
Begone!	امشى	imshi !
Begone! (out with you!)	اطلع برّا	iṭla' barra !
By all means	على كل حال	'ala kull ḥāl
Certainly	لا بدّ	la budd
,,	معلوم	ma'lūm
,,	نعم	na'am
Come back	ارجع	irja'
Come here	تعال هنا	ta'āl huna
Come in	أدخل - خش	udkhul, khushsh
Do you hear?	انت سامع	anta sāmi' ?
Do you know?	انت عارف	anta 'ārif ?
,, ,,	انت تعرف	anta ta'raf ?
Excuse me	لا تواخذنى	la tuwakhidhni
Forgive me	سامحني	sāmiḥni
From here	من هنا	min huna
Go away	روح من هنا	rūḥ min huna
Good-bye	بخاطركم	bikhāṭirkum
Good-bye (answer)	مع السلامه	ma'a-s-salāmah

Vowel sounds: hat, fāther, bit, machīne, put, rūle, aisle; **au** = **ow** in cow.
Dotted consonants, **ḥ, ḍ, ṣ, ṭ, ẓ, hard.** *See 'N.B.', p. 12.

English.	Arabic.	Pronunciation.
Go on	امشى	imshi
Give me	اعطينى	a'ṭīni
How many times?	كم مرّه	kam marrah?
Holloa there!	يا انت	ya anta!
Immediately	حالاً	ḥālan
Impossible!	ما يمكن	ma yumkin!
In front of	قدّام	quddām
In future (afterwards)	فى المستقبل	fil-mustaqbil
" "	بعدين	ba'dain
It means, that is (i.e.)	يعنى	ya'ni
Make haste	قوام - بالعجل	qawām, bil-'ajal
Many thanks	بركات ورسن	barakāt warsin
Never mind	ما عليش	ma 'alaish
No	لا	lā
Take care (look out)!	اوعَى	ū'a!
Tell me	قل لى	qull-lī
Thank you	كثر خيرك	kaththir khairak
That's another thing	هذا شى ثانى	hādha shai thāni
The sooner the better (to-day is better than to-morrow)	اليوم احسن من بكره	al-yaum aḥsan min bukrah
To the rear!	لوراء	liwara!
Very bad	ردي كثير	radi kathīr
Very much	كثير جدا	kathīr jiddan
Very nice	مليح جدًّا	malīḥ jiddan
Very often	مرّات كثيره	marrāt kathīra
Very well	طيّب مليح	taiyib malīḥ

Vowel sounds: **hat, fāther, bit, machīne, put, rūle, aisle; au = ow in cow.**
Dotted consonants, **ḥ, ḍ, ṣ, ṭ, ẓ, hard.**

ENGLISH.	ARABIC.	PRONUNCIATION.
What is this?	شو هذا	shū hādha?
What is the matter with you?	ما لك	mā lak?
Who is there?	مين هناك	mīn hunāk?
Who is this?	مين هذا	mīn hādha?
Why?	ليش ـ لماذا	laish, limādha?
Yes	نعم ـ ايوه	na'am, aiwah

Simple and Practical Phrases.

Alas!	واسفاه ـ آخّ	wa-asafāh, akhkh
Any news?	في خبر	fī khabar?
Are you in a hurry?	انت مستعجل	anta musta'jil?
Are you busy?	انت مشغول	anta mashghūl?
Are you acquainted with him?	هل تعرّفت بهِ	hal ta'arraft bihi?
As you like	على خاطرك	'ala khāṭirak
" "	على كيفك	'ala kaifak
Be quiet	إهدا	ihda
Be off	روح من هنا	rūh min huna
Bring me	جيب لي ـ هات لي	jīb li, hāt li
Bring the light here	هات النور هنا	hāt-in-nūr huna
Bring me a chair	هات لي كرسى	hāt li kursi
By-and-by	عن قريب	'an qarīb
By your leave, sir	عن اذنك يا سيدي	'an idhnak ya sīdi
Call again to-morrow	ارجع غدا	irja' ghada
Call the servant	انده الخدّام	indah-il-khaddām
Call the waiter	انده السفرجى	indah-is-sufraji
Call me early	اندهني بدري	indahni badri

Vowel sounds: hat, fāther, bit, machīne, put, rūle, aisle; **au** = **ow** in cow.
Dotted consonants, ḥ, ḍ, ṣ, ṭ, ẓ, **hard.**

English.	Arabic.	Pronunciation.
Call as you pass	زرني في مرورك	zurni fī murūrak
Can't you hear?	الا تقدر تسمع	alā taqdar tasma'?
Can it be possible?	امن الممكن	amin-il-mumkin?
Come back	ارجع	irja'
Come, be serious	تعال وكن ذا جدّ	ta'āl wakunn dhā [jadd
Come back soon	ارجع حالاً	irja' ḥālan
Come in	أدخل	udkhul
Come along	تعال	ta'āl
Come along with me	تعال معي	ta'āl ma'i
Come upstairs	طلع فوق	iṭla' fauq
Come, come, don't be [silly	تعال تعال لا تكن غبيّا	ta'āl ta'āl la takun [ghabīyan
Do not annoy me	لا تزعّلني	la tiza''ilni
Do not forget	ما تنساش	mā tinsāsh
Don't tell him	لا تقول له	la takūl luh
Do you think?	انت تفتكر	anta taftakir?
Do you understand?	انت فاهم	anta fāhim?
Do as you please	اعمل على خاطرك	i'mal 'ala khātrak
Do me the favour	اعمل معي المعروف	i'mal ma'i-l-ma'rūf
Do not be in a hurry	لا تستعجل	la tasta'jil
Don't be angry	لا تغضب	la taghḍab
Don't be long	لا تعوّق	la tat'auwaq
Do you like it?	اتحبّه	ataḥubbuh?
Don't interrupt me	لا تعطّلني عن الشغل	la tu'aṭṭilni 'ani-l-[shughl
Don't trouble yourself	لا تكلّف خاطرك	la tukallif khātrak
Don't make a noise	لا تعمل زيطه	la ta'mal zaiṭah
Did you ask him?	هل سالته	hal sa-altuh?
Don't say so	لا تقل هكذا	la takul hākadha

Vowel sounds: hat, fāther, bit, machīne, put, rūle, aisle; au = ow in cow.
Dotted consonants, ḥ, ḍ, ṣ, ṭ, ẓ, hard.

ENGLISH.	ARABIC.	PRONUNCIATION.
Get up	قوم - قم	qūm, qum
Give him	اعطيه	a'ṭīh
Give him a second time	اعطيه ثاني مرّه	a'ṭīh thāni marrah
Give me	اعطيني - اعطني	a'ṭīni, a'ṭini
Give me a different one	اعطيني غيره	a'ṭīni ghairuh
Give me a little of this	اعطيني شويه من هذا	a'ṭīni shuwaiya min hādha
Go back	ارجع	irja'
Go more slowly	امشِ على مهل	imshi 'ala mahl
Go more quickly	امشِ بالعجل	imshi bil-'ajal
Go to bed	روح نام	rūḥ nām
Good morning	صباح الخير	sabāḥu-l-khair
Good morning (answer)	يسعد صباحك	yas'id ṣabāḥak
Good day	نهارك سعيد	nahārak sa'īd
Good day (answer)	نهارك مبارك	nahārak mubārak
Good evening	مساء الخير	masā-l-khair
Good evening (answer	يسعد مساك	yas'id ma-āk
Good night	ليلتك سعيده	lailatak sa'īdah
Good night (answer)	ليلتك مباركه	lailatak mubārakah
Has the bell rung?	اندقّ الجرس	indaqqa-l-jaras?
Has the clock struck?	أدقت الساعه	a!taqqati-l-sā'ah ?
He appealed (in law)	استأنف	ista-naf
He has gone for a walk (a-walking)	راح يتنزّه	rāḥ yatanazzah
He is an excellent man	هو رجل فاضل	hū rajul fāḍil
He is a good fellow	هو جدع طيّب	hū jada' ṭaiyib
He is at dinner	هو على الغدا	hū 'ala-l-ghada

Vowel sounds: **hat, fāther, bit, machīne, put, rūle, aisle ; au = ow** in cow.
Dotted consonants, ḥ, ḍ, ṣ, ṭ, ẓ, **hard.**

English.	Arabic.	Pronunciation.
He is a clever fellow	هو جدع شاطر	hū jada' shāṭir
He is a liar	هو كذّاب	huwa kadhdhāb
He is drunk	هو سكران	huwa sakrān
He is under my orders	هو تحت امري	huwa taḥt amri
He is very angry	هو زعلان كثير	huwa za'lān kathīr
He is ill	هو عيّان	huwa 'aiyān
He learned English	تعلّم انكليزي	at'allam inglīzi
He told me	هو قال لي	huwa qāl li
Hold your tongue	أسكت - إخرس	uskut, ikhras
How do you do?	كيف حالك	kaif hālak?
" " "	كيف خاطرك	kaif khāṭirak?
How many piastres?	كم قرش	kam qirsh?
How much do you sell this for?	بكم تبيع هذا	bikam tabī' hādha?
How must we go to—?	ما هو الطريق الى—	mā hū-l-tarīq ila—?
How foolish he is!	ما احمقه	mā aḥmaquh!
I am astonished	انا متعجّب	ana mut'ajjib
I am going	انا رايح	ana rāyiḥ
I am not able	ما اقدرش	mā aqdarsh
I cannot (it is not possible for me to)	ما يمكني	mā yumkinni
I assure you	انا أحقّق لك	ana uhaqqiq lak
I have not	ما عندي	mā 'indi
I am angry with you	انا في زعل معك	ana fi za'al ma'ak
I am cold	انا بردان	ana bardān
I am hungry	انا جوعان	ana jau'ān
I am not hungry	انا مش جوعان	ana mush jau'ān

Vowel sounds: hat, fāther, bit, machīne, put, rūle, aisle; **au = ow** in cow.
Dotted consonants, ḥ, ḍ, ṣ, ṭ, ẓ, **hard.**

ENGLISH.	ARABIC.	PRONUNCIATION.
I am tired	انا تعبان	ana ta'bān
I am not accustomed [to it	انا ماليش عاده فيه	ana malīsh 'adah fīh
I am wrong	الحق عليّ	al-ḥaqq 'alaiya
I am right	الحق معى	al-ḥaqq ma'i
I cannot, am not able	ما اقدرش	mā aqdarsh
I do not care	لا أبالى	la ubāli
I do not know	لا اعرف	la a'rif
I do not speak Arabic	ما اتكلم عربى	mā atkallam 'arabi
I cannot learn Arabic if you speak English to me	ما اقدر اتعلّم عربى اذا كنت تكلمنى بالانكليزي	mā aqdar at'allam 'arabi idha kunt tu-kallimni bil-inglīzi
I have no appetite	ما لى قابليه للاكل	mā li qabliyah lil-akl
I have no passport	ما عندي تذكره	mā 'indi tadhkara
I live at —	انا ساكن في —	ana sākin fī —
I never saw him	ما شفتوش ابدًا	ma shuftūsh abadan
I want	بدّي ـ عايز	biddi, 'āyiz
I want to buy	بدّي اشتري	biddi ashtari
I am not willing	انا مش راضي	ana mush rāḍi
I am mistaken	انا غلطان	ana ghalṭān
I pray you	التمس اليك	altamis ilaika
,, ,,	بعرضك	bi'arḍak
If you please	من فضلك ـ ان شئت	min faḍlak, in shi'ta
Is it true?	اهذا صحيح	ahādha ṣaḥīḥ?
I believe not	ما اظنّ	mā aẓinn
I think it probable	اظنه محتملا	aẓunnahu muḥtamalan
It is of no consequence	لا طائل تحته	la ṭāil taḥtahu

Vowel sounds: hat, fāther, bit, machīne, put, rūle, aisle; **au = ow** in cow.
Dotted consonants, ḥ, ḍ, ṣ, ṭ, ẓ, **hard.**

English.	Arabic.	Pronunciation.
It is all one	على حدّ سوى	ʿala ḥadd siwa
Is he there ?	ياترى هو هناك	yatara huwa hunāk ?
I must go	لازم اروح	lāzim arūh
,, ,,	بودي ان اذهب	biwuddi an adhhab
I must be off [longer	لا بدّ لي من الانطلاق	la buddali mini-l-inṭi-
I must not stay any	لا اطيل المكث	la uṭīlu-l-makth [lāq
It is all over	انقضى بتمامه	inqaḍa bi tamāmu
It is finished	خلص	khalaṣ
It rains hard	تمطر قوي	tamṭur qawi
It is very warm	حرّ قوي	ḥarr qawi
Is he at home ?	ياترى هو في البيت	yatara huwa fil-bait ?
I cannot help it	لا حيله لي	la ḥīlah lī
It is the fashion	هذه هي العاده	hādhi hiya-l-ʿādah
It will strike soon	عن قريب تدقّ	ʿan qarīb taduqq
It is getting late	فات الوقت	fāta-l-waqt
I am tired of waiting	مللت من الانتظار	malalt min-il-intiẓār
Is everything ready ?	ياترى كل شى حاضر	yatara kul shai ḥāḍir ?
It is not necessary	لا يلزم	lā yalzam
It is your fault	الحق عليك	al-ḥaqq ʿalaik
It is not my fault	الحقّ مش عليّ	al-ḥaqq mush ʿallaiya
It is too late	وخري كثير	wakhri kathīr
I intend to ride	مرادي ان اركب	marādi an arkab
I believe so	ظني كذا	ẓinni kadha
It is only a report	ما هو الّا حديث	ma huwa illa ḥadīth
I have no time	ما لي وقت	ma li waqt
Is there no news ?	اليس من خبر	alais min khabar ?
,, ,, ,,	ما فيش خبر	mā fīsh khabar ?

ENGLISH.	ARABIC.	PRONUNCIATION.
I have heard none	ما سمعت شيئًا	mā samiʻtu shaian
It is time to go	حان الذهاب	ḥāna-l-dhahāb
It is rather cloudy	السمآء مغيمه	al-samā mughīmah
It is a pleasure	هذا واجب	hādha wājib
I wish you good-night	تمسي على خير	tamsi ʻala khair
I will see you again to-morrow	ساعود اراك غداً	sa-aʻūd arāk ghadan
I hope so	ان شاء اللّه	in sha-allāh
It is good for nothing	لايصلح لشي	la yaṣluḥ lishai
I don't care	لا ابالي	la ubāli
It is so, really	هذا هكذا حقّاً	hādha hākadha ḥaqqan
I will make shift without it	انا استغنى عنه	ana astaghni ʻannu
I beg your pardon (excuse me)	لا تواخذني	la tuwākhidhni
I beg your pardon (forgive me)	العفو	al-ʻafu
It is very likely	قريب الاحتمال	qarībil-iḥtimāl
It is a long way off	مسافه بعيده	masāfah baʻīdah
It is close at hand	بالقرب	bilqurb
Just as usual	حسب العاده	ḥasabi-l-ʻādah
Keep to the right	خليك على يمينك	khallīk ʻala yamīnak
Knock at the door	دقّ الباب	duqq-l-bāb
Lend me	اسلفني	aslifni
Let me alone	خلّيني	khallini
Let me help you	خلّيني اعينك	khallini uʻīnak
Lift the latch	ارفع السقاطه	irfaʻi-l-suqqāṭah
Light the candle	ولّع الشمعه	walliʻish-shamʻah

Vowel sounds: hat, fāther, bit, machīne, put, rūle, aisle; **au = ow** in cow.
Dotted consonants, ḥ, ḍ, ṣ, ṭ, ẓ, **hard.**

English.	Arabic.	Pronunciation.
Light the fire	ولع النار	walli-il-nār
Lock the door	اقفل الباب بالمفتاح	iqfili-l-bāb bilmiftāḥ
Make haste	استعجل ـ اسرع	ista'jil, isri'
Make my bed [about	اصلح فرشتي	aṣliḥ farshati
Mind what you are	انظر فيما خضت فيه	unẓur fimā khuḍta fīh
My words have made no impression on him	كلامي ما سمعوش	kalāmi mā sami'ūsh
Never mind	لاتبالِ ـ لا تكترث	la tubāli, la taktarith
,, ,,	ما عليش	mā 'alaish
No, sir	لا ياسيدي	lā yāsīdi
No, madam	لا ياستّي	lā yāsitti
Nonsense(meaningless)	بلا معنى	bila ma'na
,, (idle talk)	هذيان ـ لغو	hadhayān, laghu
Not yet	لسّا ـ بعد	lissa, ba'd
Nothing, I thank you	لا كثّر خيرك	lā, kaththir khairak
Oh, how dirty you are!	يا ما اوسخك	yā mā ausakhak!
Open the door	افتح الباب	iftaḥi-l-bāb
Open the window	افتح الشبّاك	iftaḥi-l-shubbāk
,, ,,	افتح الطاقه	iftaḥi-l-ṭāqah
Order the horses to be brought	قل لهم يُحضروا الخيل	qul lahum yuḥaḍḍi-rulkhail
Permit me	اسمح لي	ismaḥ li
,, ,,	ائذن لي	i'zin li
Permit me to accompany you	اسمح لي بان ارافقك	ismaḥ li bian urāfiqak
Pray tell me [ness	من فضلك قل لي	min faḍlak qul li
Please have the good	ان اعجبك تفضّل	in a'jabak tafaḍḍal

Vowel sounds: hat, fāther, bit, machīne, put, rūle, aisle; **au = ow** in cow.
Dotted consonants. ḥ. ḍ. ṣ. ṭ. ẓ. **hard**.

English.	Arabic.	Pronunciation.
Poor fellow!	يا مسكين	yā miskīn!
Quite sufficient	كافٍ وافٍ	kāfi wāfi
Ring the bell	دق الجرس	duqq-il-jaras
She has gone visiting	ذهبت زائره	dhahabat zāyirah
Shut the door (lock it)	اقفل الباب	iqfil-il-bāb
,, ,, (close it)	ردّ الباب	rudd-il-bāb
Sit down, please	تفضل اقعد	tafaḍḍal uqʻud
Speak plainly	تكلم واضحاً	takallam wāḍiḥan
Speak the truth	قل الحق	qul-il-ḥaqq
Stop here	انتظر هنا	intazir huna
,,	اصبر هنا	uṣbur huna
,,	استنا هنا	istanna huna
Stop a moment	اصبر لحظه	uṣbur laḥẓah
Some money	شوية دراهم	shuwaiyat darāhim
Some bread	شوية خبز	shuwaiyat khubz
Stay a little longer	امكث قليلاً ايضاً	umkuth qalīlan aiḍan
Take care, no lies	دير بالك لاتكذب	dīr bālak la takdhib
Take it	خذه	khudh-hu
Take a chair	تفضل على الكرسي	tafaḍḍal ʻalal-kursi
Take my arm	خذ بذراعي	fudh bidhirāʻi
Take an umbrella	خذ شمسيّه	fudh shamsiyah
Take me with you	خذني معك	fudhni maʻak
Take hold of the bridle	امسك اللجام	imsiki-l-lijām
Take hold of the halter	امسك الرسن	imsiki-r-rasan
Tell him	قل له	qul lu
Tell the truth	قل الصدق	quli-ṣ-ṣudq
Thank you	كثر خيرك	kathir khairak

Vowel sounds: hat, fāther, bit, machīne, put, rūle, aisle; **au=ow** in cow.
Dotted consonants, ḥ, ḍ, ṣ, ṭ, ẓ, **hard.**

English.	Arabic.	Pronunciation.
That's enough	يكفى - بسّ	yikfi, bass
There is no harm	ما في ضرر	mā fī ḍarar
They are all alike	كلهم زي بعضهم	kulluhum zai ba'ḍahum
This annoys me very much	هذا يزعلني كثير	hādha yuza''ilni kathīr
They say so	يقولون هكذا	yakūlūn hākadha
The night is dark	الليل مظلم	al-lail muẓlim
The moon shines	القمر زاهر	al-qamar zāhir
The wind is cool	الريح بارده	ar-rīḥ bāridah
Take a cloak	خذ برنس	khudh burnus
That is the whole truth	هذا الحق كله	hādha-l-ḥaqq kullu
The flies are troublesome	الدبّان مكدر	al-dubbān mukaddir
Wait here	اصبر هنا - استنا هنا	uṣbur huna, istanna huna
Wait until he comes	اصبر حتى يجي	usbur hatta yaji
Walk slowly	امش على مهلك	imshi 'ala mahlak
We will eat	بدّنا ناكل	biddana nākul
Welcome!	اهلاً وسهلاً	ahlan wasahlan!
Welcome to you!	مرحبا فيك	marḥaba fīk!
Welcome, my dear friend	مرحبا فيك يا صديقي العزيز	marḥaba fīk ya ṣadīqi-l-azīz
Well, I am satisfied	طيّب انا اكتفيت	ṭaiyib, ana iktafait
We can by no means permit it	لا نقدر ان ناذن بهِ البته	la naqdar in nādhin bihi-l-battah
We have not any cause to complain	ما لنا من علّة للشكوى	mā lana min 'illat lil-shakwa

Vowel sounds: **hat, fāther, bit, machīne, put, rūle, aisle; au = ow in cow.**
Dotted consonants, **ḥ, ḍ, ṣ, ṭ, ẓ, hard.**

English.	Arabic.	Pronunciation.
We ought to study diligently	علينا ان نجتهد في المطالعه	'alaina an najtahid fil-muṭālā'ah
What are you doing?	شو تعمل	shu ta'mal?
What did he say?	شو اللي قاله	shu illi kālu?
What does it contain?	شو فيه	shu fīh?
What do you say?	شو بتقول	shu bitqūl?
What do you mean?	شو معناك	shu ma'nāk?
What do you want?	شو بدّك	shu biddak?
What have you got?	شو عندك	shu 'indak?
What is this—that?	شو هذا	shu hādha?
What is the difference?	شو الفرق	shu-l-farq?
What a pity!	يا خساره	ya khisārah!
What kind of man is he?	اي الناس هو	ai-ul-nās huwa?
What a wonder!	يا عجباً	ya 'ajaban!
What is the matter?	شو المادّه	shu-l-māddah?
What is the news?	شو الخبر	shu-l-khabar?
What is to be done?	شو العمل	shu-l-'amal?
What is your name?	شو اسمك	shu ismak?
What is your opinion?	شو رايك	shu rāyak?
What makes you angry?	شو اللي يزعلك	shu illi yuza''ilak?
What o'clock is it?	شو الساعه	shu-l-sā'ah?
What pay does he get?	كم ماهيّته	kam mahiyatu?
What shall I do?	شو اعمل	shu a'mal?
What time is it?	كم الوقت	kam-il-waqt?
What is the matter with you? [him?	ما لك	mā lak?
What do you think of	ما ظنك فيه	mā ẓinak fīh?

Vowel sounds: **hat, fāther, bit, machīne, put, rūle, aisle; au = ow** in cow.
Dotted consonants, **ḥ, ḍ, ṣ, ṭ, ẓ, hard.**

English.	Arabic.	Pronunciation.
Where are you going?	اين ذاهب انت	ain dhāhib int?
Where do you live?	فين ساكن انت	fain sākin int?
Where is he now?	فين هو الان	fain hu alān?
Well done!	ما شاء الله	ma shā-Allāh!
Which house is yours?	انهو بيتك	anhū baitak?
Which horse will you ride?	اي حصان تركب	ai ḥisān tarkab?
Will you take anything?	آلا تاخذ شيئاً	alā tākhudh shaian?
Where is the lamp?	اين القنديل	ain-al-qandīl?
Will you be engaged?	اتكون مشغولاً	atakūn mashghūlan?
Without joking	بلا مزاح	bala mizāḥ
Where did you get it?	من اين حصلته	min ain ḥaṣṣaltu?
Where does he live?	اين يسكن هو	ain yaskun huwa?
Where is she?	اين هي	ain hiya?
When will you go hence?	متى تذهب من هنا	mata tadhhab min huna?
Will you allow me?	اتسمح لي	atasmaḥ li?
Will you oblige me?	اتعمل معي معروف	ata'mal ma'i ma'rūf?
Will you take this?	أتاخذ هذا	atākhudh hādha?
Who told you?	من قال لك	man qāl lak?
You will oblige me	تجعلني ممنونا	taj'alni mamuūnan
You must go now	لازم تروح الان	lāzim tarūḥ alān
You are late	انت تأخرت	anta ta-akhkhart
You are right	الحق معك	al-ḥaqq ma'ak
You are wrong	الحق عليك	al-ḥaqq 'alaik
You are very kind	فضلك علينا	faḍlak 'alaina
You walk too fast	انت تمشي بعجله زائده	anta tamshi bi'ajalah zāyidah

English.	Arabic.	Pronunciation.
You come with me	انت تجي معي	anta taji ma‘i
You are too young	انت صغير كثير	anta ṣaghīr kathīr
You must dress well	لازم تلبس طيّب	lazim tilbis taiyib
You must be quick	لازم تستعجل	lazim tasta‘jīl
You are ready now	انت حاضر الان	anta ḥādir alān

Arrival.

English.	Arabic.	Pronunciation.
I want a boat	عايز فلوكه	āyiz fulukah
This is not big enough for us	هذه مش كبيره بالكفايه لنا	bādhi mush kabīrah bil-kifayah lana
No, it will not do	لا ما تنفع	lā, mā tanfa‘
Can you take our luggage with you?	أتقدر تاخذ عفشنا معك	ataqdar tākhudh ‘afshana ma‘ak ?
Certainly, sir	نعم يا سيدي	na‘am ya sīdi
I will bring you a porter	اجيب لك عتّال	ajīb lak ‘attāl
He can carry the lot by himself, he is strong	يقدر يحمل الكل وحده هو قوي	yaqdar yaḥmil - ul - kull waḥdu, huwa qawi
He has a cart too	عنده كمان عربيّة حمل	‘indu kamān ‘arabīyat [ḥiml
There is first the custom-house examination	اولاً في تفتيش الكمرك	auwalan fī taftīsh-ul-kumruk
We will go in the carriage	نحن نروح في العربيّه	naḥn narūḥ fil arabīya
You must come with us	لازم تجي معنا	lāzim taji ma‘na
Tell me how much the fare is	قل لي كم الاجره	qul li kam-l-ujrah

Vowel sounds: **hat, fāther, bit, machīne, put, rūle, aisle; au = ow** in cow.
Dotted consonants, ḥ, ḍ, ṣ, ṭ, ẓ, **hard.**

English.	Arabic.	Pronunciation.
How much is the fare to the station?	كم الاجره للمحطه	kam-l-ujrah lilma-ḥaṭṭa?
Each person four piastres	كل شخص اربعة قروش	kul shakhṣ arba'at qurūsh
And the porter how much?	والعتّال كم	wal-'attāl kam?
He is entitled to ask two piastres, and is asking for baqshish because it is hot and the luggage is heavy	حقّه قرشين وطالب بخشيش لان الدنيا شوب والعفش ثقيل	ḥaqqu qirshain waṭā-lib bakhshīsh, lian-id-dunya shaub wal-'afsh thaqīl
Is the luggage correct?	ياترى العفش تمام	yatara-l-'afsh tamām?
Eleven pieces	احدى عشر رزمه	iḥda 'shar razma
You left one in the steamer	خلّيت واحدة في المركب	khallait waḥida fil-'markab
You must send the porter to inquire about it	لازم ترسل العتّال يسال عنها	lāzim tursilu-l-'attāl yas-al 'anha
I quite forgot it, sir	نسيتها بالتمام ياسيدي	nasaituha bit-tamā. ya sīdi
Thank goodness! some one is bringing it now	الحمد لله واحد جايبها الان	al-ḥamdu lillāh waḥad jāyibha alān

The Railway.

Is the station far?	ياترى المحطه بعيده	yatara al-maḥaṭṭa ba'īda?
No; a quarter of an hour's distance only	لا مسافه ربع ساعه فقط	lā; masāfat rub' sā'ah faqaṭ

ENGLISH.	ARABIC.	PRONUNCIATION.
When does the train go?	متى يسافر القطار	mata yusāfiru-l-qitār?
In half an hour	بعد نصّ ساعه	ba'd nuṣṣ sā'ah
Anyhow, it will not start before the mails come	على كل حال ما يقوم قبل ان تجي البوسطه	'ala kull ḥāl mā yaqūm qabl in taji-l-bōsṭa
We need not hurry	لا لزوم للعجله	lā luzūm lil-'ajalah
Please go and get the tickets	من فضلك روح وجيب التذاكر	min faḍlak rūḥ wajībi-l-tadhākir
I want four first-class	عايز اربع محلات درجه أولى	'āyiz arba' maḥallāt darajaūla
There is a ticket short	ناقصة تذكرة واحدة	naqiṣa tadhkara wāḥida
Never mind! I will bring you another	ما عليش اجيب لك واحده ثانيه	mā 'alaish ajīb lak wāḥida thāniyah
And the money: is it right?	والدراهم أهي تمام	wad-darāhim ahī tamām?
One piastre is bad	قرش واحد بطّال	qirsh wāḥid baṭṭāl
(By the life of your father) I swear, it is good	وحياة ابوك هو طيّب	waḥayāt abūk huwa taiyib
You are right, it is only old	الحق معك هو بس قديم	al-ḥaqq ma'ak huwa bass qadīm
I would like to ask the interpreter	احبّ اسأل الترجمان	aḥubb as-al at-turjumān
There is no need to	ما فيش لزوم	ma fīsh luzūm
I will ascertain from him all the same	مع ذلك اريد استعلم منه	ma' dhālik urīd asta'-līm minhu

Vowel sounds · hat, fāther, bit, machīne, put, rūle, aisle; **au**=ow in cow.
Dotted consonants, ḥ, ḍ, ṣ, ṭ, ẓ, **hard.**

ENGLISH.	ARABIC.	PRONUNCIATION.
The luggage goes without extra charge	العفش يروح بلاش	al-'afsh yarūḥ balāsh
No! I have paid 15 piastres: here is the receipt	لا انا دفعت خمسةعشر قرش ها هو الوصل	lā, ana dafa't khamsata'shar qirsh: hā huwa-l-waṣl
I wish you a good journey	مع السلامه بحفظ الله	ma'as-salāmah biḥifẓ-il-lāh
You are travellers	حضرتكم مسافرين	ḥaḍratkum musāfirīn
How long have you been in Egypt?	كم صار لكم في بر مصر	kam ṣār lakum fī barr Masr?
We arrived only to day	وصلنا اليوم فقط	waṣalna-l-yaum faqaṭ
Are you going to Jerusalem?	ياترى رايحين الى القدس	yatara rāyiḥīn ilal-quds?
We shall stay there four days, waiting for a friend	نقيم فيها اربعة ايام ننتظر صاحب لنا	nuqīm fīha arba'at aiyām nantaẓir ṣāḥib lana
It is not enough; you require two or three weeks at least	ما يكفيش يلزمكم جمعتين او ثلاثة على الاقلّ	mā yakfīsh yalzamkum jum'atain au thalātha 'alal-aqall
Our intention is to see everything before we go back to England	قصدنا نشوف كل شي قبل ما نرجع الى بلاد الانكليز	qaṣduna nashūf kull shai qabl mā narja' ila bilādi-l-inglīz
Good; perhaps I shall see you when you return from Bethlehem	طيّب ان شاء الله اشوفكم لما ترجعوا من بيت لحم	aiyib; insha-Allāh ashūfkum lamma tarja'u min Bait-luḥm
Please God!	ان شاء الله	insha-Allāh!

Vowel sounds: hat, fāther, bit, machīne, put, rūle, aisle; **au = ow in cow.**
Dotted consonants, ḥ, ḍ, ṣ, ṭ, ẓ, **hard.**

The Hotel.

ENGLISH.	ARABIC.	PRONUNCIATION.
Where is the proprietor of the hotel?	اين صاحب اللوكانده	ain ṣāḥib-l-lūkāndah?
Have you a room vacant?	ياترى عندك اوضه فاضيه	yatara 'indak auḍah fāḍiyah?
This room is very small	هذه الاوضه صغيره جدًّا	hādhi-l-auḍah ṣaghīrah jiddan
Have you a large room?	هل عندك اوضه كبيره	hal 'indak auḍah kabīrah?
Show me a bedroom.	ارني اوضة نوم	arini auḍat naum
I will take this one	اخذ هذه	ākhudh hādhi
Have you no better rooms?	ما عندك اوض احسن	mā 'indak uwaḍ aḥsan?
I want a large one	عايز واحدة كبيرة	'āyiz wāḥida kabīra
Are you the landlord?	انت صاحب اللوكانده	anta ṣāḥib-l-lūkāndah?
How much do you charge per day?	كم تطلب في اليوم	kam taṭlub fi-l-yaum?
Has my luggage come?	هل جاء عفشي	hal jā 'afshi?
Take the luggage upstairs	إطلع العفش فوق	iṭli'-l-'afsh fauq
Put it down here	نزّله هنا	nazzilu huna
I want something to eat	اريد شي للاكل	arīd shai lil-akl
Anything will do	ايش ما كان طيّب	aish mā kāu ṭaiyib
Give me the key of my room	اعطيني مفتاح اوضتي	a'tīni miftāḥ auḍati

Vowel sounds: hat, fāther, bit, machīne, put, rūle, aisle; **au**=ow in cow. *Dotted consonants,* ḥ, ḍ, ṣ, ṭ, ẓ, **hard.**

ENGLISH.	ARABIC.	PRONUNCIATION.
What are the meal-times?	ما هي ساعات الاكل	mā hī sā'āt-l-akl?
Lunch is at . . . and dinner at . . .	الغدا الساعه . . . والعشا الساعه . . .	alghada assā'ah . . . wal'asha assā'ah . . .
There is no fixed time	ما في وقت مقرّر	mā fī waqt muqarrar
And breakfast?	والفطور	wal-fuṭūr?
Can I dine in my room?	أيمكنّي اتغدا في اوضتي	ayumkinni atghadda fī auḍati?
Where is the w.c.?	فين بيت الراحة	fain bait-l-rāḥah?
I want a warm bath	عايز حمام سخن	'āyiz ḥammām sukhun
Give me a piece of soap	اعطيني شقفة صابون	a'ṭīni shaqfat ṣābūn
Give me a towel	اعطيني منشفه	a'ṭīni minshafah
Where is the bell?	فين الجرس	fain-l-jaras?
I want a candle	عايز شمعه	'āyiz sham'ah
I think of leaving to-morrow	انوي الذهاب بكره	anwi-l-dhahāb bukrah
Call me early in the morning	صحّيني بدري في الصباح	ṣaḥḥīni badri fiṣ-ṣabāḥ
Call my servant	نادي خادمي	nādi khādimi
Take me to the station	خذني للمحطه	khudhni lil-maḥaṭṭah

Meals.

(For Vocabulary, see p. 34.)

Please bring tea and cakes	من فضلك جيب شاي وكعك	min faḍlak jīb shāi waqa'q
Bring bread and butter	جيب خبز وزبده	jīb khubz wa-zibdah

Vowel sounds: hat, fāther, bit, machīne, put, rūle, aisle; **au=ow** in cow.
Dotted consonants, ḥ, ḍ, ṣ, ṭ, ẓ, **hard.**

ENGLISH.	ARABIC.	PRONUNCIATION.
Another cup of tea	فنجان شاي ثانٍ	finjān shāi thāni
Give me some more sugar (milk)	اعطيني كمان سكر (حليب)	a'ṭīni kamān sukkar (ḥalīb)
Put some more water in the teapot	حط زيادة ماء في ابريق الشاي	ḥuṭṭ ziyādat mā fī ibrīq-l-shāi
This is enough	هذا يكفي	hādha yakfi
May I offer you some fish?	هل اقدم لك شوية سمك	hal uqaddim lak shuwayat samak?
Thanks, I will take some	كثر خيرك اخذ شويّه	kaththir khairak ākhudh shuwaiyah
Which of them do you prefer?	ايهما تُفضّل	aiyuhuma tufaḍḍil?
I prefer roast to boiled	أُفضّل المحمّر على المسلوق	ufaḍḍil-l-muḥammar 'ala-l-maslūq
Is there any fish here?	ياترى في سمك هنا	yatara fī samak huna?
There is none	لا يوجد شي	lā yūjad shai
Tell the cook to make soup	قل للطباخ يعمل شوربه	qul lil-ṭabbākh ya'mal shaurabah
He is not a good cook	هو مش طباخ شاطر	huwa 'mush ṭabbākh shāṭir
I have nothing to eat	ما في عندي شى للاكل	mā fī 'indi shai lil-akl
Is the soup ready?	هل الشوربة حاضره	hal-il-shaurabah ḥāḍirah?
Dinner is ready	العشاء حاضر	al-'asha ḥāḍir
Do you like . . . ?	هل تحب . . .	hal tuḥibb . . . ?
If it is fresh	ان كان طازه	in kān ṭazah

Vowel sounds: **hat, fāther, bit, machīne, put, rūle, aisle; au = ow in cow.**
Dotted consonants, **ḥ, ḍ, ṣ, ṭ, ẓ, hard.**

English.	Arabic.	Pronunciation.
Give me a little, please	اعطيني شويه من فضلك	aʿṭīnī shuwaiyah min faḍlak
Will you pass the mustard?	من فضلك ناولني الخردل	min faḍlak nāwilni-l-khardal
Pass me the sauce	ناولني المرقه	nāwilni-l-maraqah
Waiter, some bread	يا سفرجي شوية خبز	ya-sufraji shuwaiyat khubz
What wine will you take, sir?	اي نبيذ تشرب ياسيدي	ai nabīdh tashrab ya-sīdi?
Show me the wine list	وريني قايمة النبيذ	warrīni qāyimat-l-nabīdh
Have you English beer?	في عندك بيرا انكليزية	fī ʿindak bīra inglizīyah?
Open the bottle	افتح القنينه	iftaḥ-il-qannīnah
Is this water filtered?	ياترى هذا الماء مصفى	yatara hādha-l-mā muṣaffa?
Is it good for drinking?	هل يصلح للشرب	hal yaṣlaḥ lil-shurb?
Change my plate	غير صحني	ghaiyir ṣaḥni

Correspondence, Post, Telegrams, etc.

(For Vocabulary, see p. 47.)

Have no letters come for me?	ما جاءت لي مكاتيب	ma jā-at lī makātīb?
No, none have come	لا ما جا شي	lā ma jā shai
He ought to be here by now	يجب ان يكون هنا الان	yajib an yakūn huna al-ān
I have heard nothing	ما سمعت شي	mā samiʿt shai

ENGLISH.	ARABIC.	PRONUNCIATION.
Has the mail steamer arrived?	ياترى وصل وابور البوسطه	yatara wasal wābūr-ul-bōsṭa?
Go and see if the mail is in	روح وشوف ان كانت البوسطه وصلت	rūḥ washūf in kānat-il-bōsṭa waṣalat
Are there any letters for me?	في مكاتيب لي	fī makātīb lī?
I have not received any [letters	ما استلمت مكاتيب	ma istalamt makātīb
Please forward my letters to . . .	من فضلك ارسل مكاتيبي الى . . .	min faḍlak irsil makā-tībi ila . . .
Please weigh this letter	من فضلك اوزن هذا المكتوب	min faḍlak ūzan hādha-l-maktūb
How much is the postage on these letters?	كم اجره بوسطة هذه المكاتيب	kam ujrat bōsṭat hādhi-l-makātīb?
Can you lend me a pen?	تقدر تسلفني قلم .	taqdar tusallifni qalam?
Have you a lead pencil?	هل عندك قلم رصاص	hal ʻindak qalam riṣāṣ?
I want some note-paper	عايز ورق كتابه	ʻāyiz waraq kitābah
Give me an envelope	اعطيني ظرف	aʻṭīni ẓarf
Where is the ink?	فين الحبر	fain-il-ḥibr?
Lend me a piece of blotting-paper	سلفني ورقة نشافه	sallifni warakat nashshāfah
Give me some stamps	اعطيني بعض طوابع بوسطة	aʻṭīni baʻḍ ṭawabiʻ bōsṭa
Tell him to wait	قل له ينتظر	qul luh yantaẓir
I will send a reply later	ارسل الجواب بعدين	ursil-ul-jawāb baʻdain

Vowel sounds: **hat, fāther, bit, machīne, put, rūle, aisle; au = ow in cow.**
Dotted consonants, **ḥ, ḍ, ṣ, ṭ, ẓ, hard.**

English.	Arabic.	Pronunciation.
Can I send a telegram?	ياترى يمكني ارسل تلغراف	yatara yumkinni ursil teleghrāf?
I have received a telegram from . . .	وصلني تلغراف من . . .	waṣalni teleghrāf min . . .
I want a postal order	عايز حوالة بوسطه	ʻayiz hawālat bōsṭa
The payee's name and address are . . .	اسم المودى اليه وعنوانه هما . . .	ism-ul-muwadda ilaih wa-ʻanwānuh huma . . .
I am the sender	انا المرسل	ana-l-mursil
Please cash this money order	من فضلك اعطيني صرف هذه الحواله	min faḍlak aʻṭīni sarf hādhi-l-ḥawālah
This letter is to be registered	هذا المكتوب للتسجيل	hādha-l-maktūb lil-tasjīl
Registered letter	مكتوب مسوكر	maktūb musaukar
Give me a receipt for it	اعطيني بهِ وصل	aʻṭīni bihi waṣl

Shopping.

I want some silk	عايز شويه حرير	ʻayiz shuwayat ḥarīr
This silk is very dear	هذا الحرير غالي كثير	hādha-l-ḥarīr ghāli kathīr
This material wears well	هذا القماش يدوم زمان طويل	hādha-l-qumāsh yadūm zamān ṭawīl
I will guarantee it	انا اضمنه	ana aḍmanuh
I don't guarantee it	انا لا اضمنه	ana lā aḍmanuh
Please show me some gloves	من فضلك فرّجني على بعض كفوف	min faḍlak farrijni ʻala baʻḍ kufūf

English.	Arabic.	Pronunciation.
I want a cross made of olive-wood	عايز صليب مصنوع من خشب زيتون	'ayiz ṣalīb maṣnū' min khashab zaitūn
Also flowers from Bethlehem	كمان زهور من بيت لحم	kamān zuhūr min Baitlaḥm
I want to see that desk [price?	عايز اشوف تلك المكتبه	'ayiz ashūf tilk-il-maktabah
What is the lowest	ما هو السعر الادنى	mā hū-l-si'r-ul-adna ?
Is this frame expensive?	ياترى هذا البرواز غالي	yatara hādha-l-burwāz ghāli ?
I will select the best from among these	انتخب الاحسن بين هذه	antakhib-ul-aḥsan bain hādhi
I want to see some curios	عايز اشوف بعض انتيكات	'ayiz ashūf ba'ḍ antikāt
Are they genuine?	هل هي حقيقيه	hal hī ḥaqīqiyah ?
May I show it to you?	تسمح لي اوريك اياها	tasmaḥ li uwarrīk iyāha ?
Please give me about ten	من فضلك اعطيني نحو عشره	min faḍlak a'ṭīni naḥu 'asharah
These suit me, but the price is too high	هذه توافقني لكن السعر غالي كثير	hādhi tuwafiqni lākin-is-si'r ghāli kathīr
I don't want any more	مش عايز اكثر	mush 'ayiz akthar
It is dearer than I thought	انها اغلى مما افتكرت	innaha aghla mimma iftakart
These are cheaper	هذه ارخص	hādhi arkhaṣ
These are still better	هذه كمان احسن	hādhi kamān aḥsan
How much do you ask for them?	كم تطلب فيها	kam taṭlub fīha ?

Vowel sounds : **hat, fāther, bit, machīne, put, rūle, aisle; au = ow in cow.**
Dotted consonants, **ḥ, ḍ, ṣ, ṭ, ẓ, hard.**

ENGLISH.	ARABIC.	PRONUNCIATION.
I can't let you have them for less	لا يمكنني اسمح لك بها بقل	lā yumkinni asmaḥ lak biha bi-aqall
I will buy these	اشتري هذه	ashtari hādhi
How do you like these?	كيف تحب هذه	kaif tuḥib hādhi?
I don't like any of these	لا احب واحده منها	lā uḥib wāḥida minha
Do you want anything else?	هل ترغب في شي اخر	hal targhab fi shai akhar?
Send the things to my hotel	ارسل الاشياء الى لوكاندتي	arsil - il - ashya ila lukāndati
What name, sir?	ما الاسم يا سيدي	mā-l-ism yā sīdi?

An Excursion.

Wake me early in the morning	صحّيني بدري في الصباح	ṣaḥḥīni badri fiṣ-ṣabāḥ
We are going to see the Mount of Olives to-morrow	رايحين نشوف جبل الزيتون بكره	rāyiḥīn nashūf jabal-al-zaitūn bukra
Do you want me to get the donkeys ready?	أتريد ان احضر الحمير	aturīd an uḥaḍḍiru-l-ḥamīr?
Perhaps we shall go in a carriage, but anyhow we shall take food with us	ربما نركب عربيّه ولكن على كل حال ناخذ معنا اكل	rubbama narkab ʻarabiyah, walākin ʻala kull ḥāl nākhudh maʻna akl
Yes, sir; everything will be all right	نعم يا سيدي كل شيء يكون بالتمام	naʻam ya sīdi kull shai yakūn bittamām
You must take the necessaries for tea	لازم تاخذ لوازم الشاي	lāzim tākhudh lawā-zim-l-shāi

Vowel sounds: hat, fāther, bit, machīne, put, rūle, aisle; au = ow in cow.
Dotted consonants, ḥ, ḍ, ṣ, ṭ, ẓ, **hard.**

ENGLISH.	ARABIC.	PRONUNCIATION.
The teapot, the spirit, matches, and everything must be wrapped in paper	ابريق الشاي والسبرتو والكبريت وكل شي' لازم يلتفّ بالورق	ibrīqu-sh-shāi wal-sbiritu, wal-kabrīt, wakull shai lāzim yaltaff bil-waraq
I have wrapped up everything and put it into the basket	لفّيت كل شي' وحطّيته في السلّه	laffait kull shai wa-ḥattaitu fis-salla
We can buy oranges and melons on the way	يمكنا نشتري برتقان وبطّيخ ونحن في الطريق	yumkinna nashtari burtuqān wabaṭṭīkh wanahnu fiṭ-tarīq
Good; do not forget the wine	طيّب لا تنسَ النبيذ	taiyib la tansa-l-nabīdh
We want to go up the minaret	نريد نطلع لفوق المأذنه	nārīd naṭla' lifauqi-l-mā-dhana
Just as you wish, sir; it is not difficult, but it tires one	على خاطرك يا خواجا ما في صعوبه ولكن الانسان يتعب	'ala khāṭirak ya khawāja; mā fi su'ūba, walākini-l-insān yat'ab
I will bring a permit for you all to go up	اجيب رُخصه لكلكم لتطلعوا	ajīb rukhṣa likullikum litaṭla'u
This is necessary	هذه ضروريّه	hādhi ḍrūriyah
It will cost two piastres each	ثمنها قرشين عن كل شخص	thamanha qirshain 'an kull shakhṣ
Is the lady strong, and can she also go up?	ياترى الست قويّه وتقدر تطلع كمان	yatara-l-sit kawiyah wataqdar taṭla' kamān?
Get the tea ready at once	حضّر الشاي حالاً	ḥaḍḍiri-sh-shāi ḥālan

Vowel sounds: **hat, fāther, bit, machīne, put, rūle, aisle; au = ow in cow.**
Dotted consonants, **ḥ, ḍ, ṣ, ṭ, ẓ, hard.**

English.	Arabic.	Pronunciation.
The horse is going lame, and is very tired	لحصان يعرج وتعبان كثير	al-hiṣān ya'ruj watā'-bān kathīr
The driver is beating the horse without any reason	العربجي عمال يضرب الحصان بدون سبب	al-'arbaji 'ammal yaḍrubu-l-hiṣān bidūn sabab
He knows his business	يعرف شغله	ya'rif shughlu
He is not cruel	هو مش قاسي	huwa mush qāsi
Another time I will take some one else	المرّه الثانيه اخذ واحد غيره	al-marra-th-thāniya ākhudh wāḥad ghairu
They are all alike	كلهم مثل بعضهم البعض	kulluhum mithl ba'ḍahumi-l-ba'ḍ
Have you made an account of what you have spent?	هل عملت جساب الدراهم اللي صرفتها	hal 'amilt ḥisāba-d-darāhim illi saraf-taha?
I have spent three Turkish liras, four mejidis, and fifteen piastres	صرفت ثلاثة ليرات عثمانيه واربع مجيديات وخمسةعشر قرش	ṣaraft thalāthat lirāt 'uthmānīyah wa-arba' majīdiyat wa-khamsat 'ashar qirsh
I hope you, sir, the ladies, and the other gentlemen have enjoyed yourselves to-day	عسى ان حضرتكم يا سيدي والستات والخواجات الثانيين انبسطتم اليوم	'asa in haḍratkum ya sīdi was-sittāt wal-khawajātu-th-thāniyīn inbasaṭ-tum-l-yaum
We all enjoyed our excursion, only the ladies are a little tired	كلنا انبسطنا في سفرتنا القصيره فقط الستات تعبانات شويه	kulluna inbasaṭna fi safratna-l-qaṣīra, faqaṭi-s-sittāt ta'bānāṭ shuwaiyah

Passages of Arabic with Pronunciation and Translation interlined.

1. "The Lord's Prayer" (Matt. vi, 9–13).

ٱسْمُكَ	لِيَتَقَدَّسِ	ٱلسَّمٰوَاتِ	فِي	ٱلَّذِي	أَبَانَا
-s-muka	liyataqaddasi	-s-samawāt	fī	-l-ladhi	abāna
Thy name	hallowed be	the heavens	in	which art	our Father

ٱلسَّمَاءِ	فِي	كَمَا	مَشِيئَتُكَ	لِتَكُنْ	مَلَكُوتُكَ	لِيَأْتِ
-s-samā'i	fī	kama	mashī'atuka	litakun	malakūtuka	liya'ti
the heaven	in	as	Thy will	be done	Thy kingdom	come

أَعْطِنَا	كَفَافَنَا	خُبْزَنَا	ٱلْأَرْضِ	عَلَى	كَذٰلِكَ
a'ṭina	kafāfana	khubzana	-l-arḍi	'ala	kadhālika
give us	sufficient for us	our bread	the earth	upon	so

نَحْنُ	نَغْفِرُ	كَمَا	ذُنُوبَنَا	لَنَا	وَٱغْفِرْ	ٱلْيَوْمَ
naḥnu	naghfiru	kama	dhunūbana	lana	waghfir	-l-yauma
we	forgive	as	our trespasses	us	and forgive	to-day

فِي	تُدْخِلْنَا	وَلَا	إِلَيْنَا	أَسَاءَ	لِمَنْ
fī	tudkhilna	wa-lā	ilaina	asā'a	liman
into	lead us	and not	against us	trespassed	to them who

لِأَنَّ	ٱلشِّرِّيرِ	مِنَ	نَجِّنَا	لٰكِنْ	تَجْرِبَةٍ
lianna	-sh-shirrīri	mina	najjina	lākin	tajribatin
for that	the evil one	from	deliver us	but	temptation

وَٱلْمَجْدَ	وَٱلْقُوَّةَ	ٱلْمُلْكَ	لَكَ
wal-majda	wal-quwata	-l-mulka	laka
and the glory	and the power	the kingdom	to Thee belongeth

آمِينَ .	ٱلْآبَدِ	إِلَى
āmīn	-l-abadi	ila
amen	the eternity	to

2. Qur'ān (Koran), chap. iv, verse 169.

فِي	تَغْلُوا	لَا	ٱلْكِتَابِ	أَهْلَ	يَا
fī	taghlu	lā	-l-kitābi	ahla	yā
in	commit extravagance	not	of the book	people	O

ٱلْحَقَّ	إِلَّا	ٱللّٰهِ	عَلَى	تَقُولُوا	وَلَا	دِينِكُم
-l-ḥaqqa	illa	-l-llāhi	'ala	taqūlu	wa-lā	dīnikum'
the truth	except	God	of	speak	and not	your religion

رَسُولُ	مَرْيَمَ	ٱبْنُ	عِيسَى	ٱلْمَسِيحُ	إِنَّمَا
rasūlu	Maryama	-bnu	'īsa	-l-Masīḥu	innamā
is the apostle	of Mary	the son	Jesus	the Christ	for verily

مَرْيَمَ	إِلَى	أَلْقَاهَا	وَكَلِمَتُهُ	ٱللّٰهِ
Maryama	ila	alqāha	wa-kalimatuhū	-l-llāhi
Mary	into	which He conveyed	and his Word	of God

بِٱللّٰهِ	فَآمِنُوا	مِنْهُ	وَرُوحٌ
bil-llāhi	fa-āminu	minhu	wa-rūḥun
in God	therefore believe	from Himself	and a Spirit

ثَلَاثَةٌ	تَقُولُوا	وَلَا	وَرُسُلِهِ
thalāthatun	taqūlu	wa-lā	wa-rusulihi
a Trinity	say	and not	and His apostles

Idiomatic translation of the above:—

O people of the Book! commit no extravagance in your religion; and speak not of God except the truth. For verily Christ Jesus, the son of Mary, is the apostle of God, and His Word which He conveyed into Mary, and a Spirit, *proceeding* from Himself. Believe therefore in God and His apostles, and say not "a Trinity".

MONEY.

Turkish Government Currency used in Syria, with the English and American equivalents.

Gold Coins.

		Piastres.			English. £	s.	d.		American. Dollars.
2½ līra	=	250	. . . =	about	2	5	1	=	10·91
Līra 'Uthmānīyah [1]	=	100	. . . =	,,		18	0¾	=	4·36
½ līra	=	50	. . . =	,,		9	1	=	2·18
¼ līra	=	25	. . . =	,,		4	6½	=	1·09
Also in circulation [2]—									
Līra Inglizīyah [3]	=	110	. . . =		1	0	0	=	4·85
Līra Faransawīyah [4]	=	88	. . . =	about		16	0	=	3·88

Silver Coins.

		Piastres.	Paras. [6]			£	s.	d.		Dollars.
Majīdi	=	20	. . .	=	about		3	7	=	0·87
Nusf Majīdi	=	10	. . .	=	,,		1	9½	=	0·43
Zihrawi	=	6	. . .	=	,,		1	1	=	0·26
Rub' Majīdi	=	5	. . .	=	,,			10¾	=	0·21
2 piastres	=	2	. . .	=	,,			4¼	=	0·08
Piastre [5]	=		40	=	,,			2¼	=	0·04
Also in circulation [2]—										
Shilling	=	5	20	=	,,		1	0	=	0·25
Franc	=	4	10	=	,,			9½	=	0·19

In addition *nickel* coins of 20 and 10 paras and *bronze* coins of 10 and 5 paras are current. (40 paras = 1 piastre.)

N.B. All Government taxes and dues are paid according to this fixed standard, but the value of the above in piastres varies greatly in the different provinces for all other payments. This applies also to railway fares.

Credit notes can be cashed in English gold.

English and American money with the Turkish equivalents.

English. £	s.	d.		American. Dollars.		Turkish. Piastres.	Paras.
50	0	0	=	242·50	=	5,500	0
25	0	0	=	121·25	=	2,750	0
10	0	0	=	48·50	=	1,100	0
5	0	0	=	24·25	=	550	0

[1] Turkish pound. [2] But not recognized currency. [3] English sovereign.
[4] French Napoleon. [5] Arabic *qirsh*, pl. *qurūsh*. [6] Arabic *bāra*, pl. *bārāt*.

English.				American.		Turkish.	
£	*s.*	*d.*		*Dollars.*		*Piastres.*	*Paras.*
4	0	0	=	19·40	=	440	0
3	0	0	=	14·55	=	330	0
1	0	0	=	4·85	=	110	0
	10	0	=	2·42	=	55	0
	5	0	=	1·21	=	27	20
	4	0	=	·97	=	22	0
	2	6	=	·60	=	13	30
	2	0	=	·48	=	11	0
	1	0	=	·24	=	5	20
		6	=	·12	=	2	30
		3	=	·06	=	1	15
		1	=	·02	=	0	18
		0½	=	·01	=	0	9
		0¼	=	(½ cent)	=	0	4

WEIGHTS AND MEASURES.

Weight.

114 dirhams or 96 mithqāls make 1 ratl or pound = ·99 lb. av. English = about 12 oz. 8½ dr.

100 ratl make 1 qanṭār = 78·375 lb. av. English = about 2 qr. 22 lb. 6 oz.

The oqqa is 400 dirhams = 2·75 lb. av. English = 2 lb. 12 oz.

Length.

1 qaṣabah = 11 ft. 7·76 in. English.

1 pik (dira'), the principal measure for cloth and silk = 26·8 English inches.

Surface.

The faddān, or acre, is 400 square qaṣabah = 1 acre 6 roods.

Capacity.

24 rub's make 1 ardab = 5·44 bushels (1 pk. 1 gal. 2 qts.).

POSTAL RATES.

The postage on *letters* from Syria to England, America, and other countries in the Postal Union is at the rate of 1 piastre (about 2¼*d.*) for 15 grams (about ½ oz.); *postcards*, 20 paras (about 1*d.*); *newspapers*, 10 paras (about ½*d.*) for 50 grams.

The inland rates on *letters* (*a*) for places on the sea-coast, 20 paras (about 1*d.*) for 15 grams; (*b*) for the interior, 1 piastre (about 2¼*d.*) for 15 grams; on *postcards*, 20 paras (about 1*d.*); *newspapers*, 5 paras (about ¼*d.*) for 30 grams.